Bridging Cultural Barriers for Corporate Success

Bridging Cultural Barriers for Corporate Success

How to Manage the Multicultural Work Force

Sondra Thiederman, Ph.D.

Lexington Books
D.C. Heath and Company/Lexington, Massachusetts/Toronto

1991

Library of Congress Cataloging-in-Publication Data

Thiederman, Sondra B.
   Bridging cultural barriers for corporate success : how to manage the
multicultural work force / Sondra Thiederman.
      p.   cm.
   Includes bibliographical references.
   Includes index.
   ISBN 0-669-21930-4 (alk. paper)
   1. Communication in personnel management—United
States—Cross-cultural studies.   2. Personnel management—United
States—Cross-cultural studies.   3. Intercultural communication—United
States.
   I. Title.
   HF5549.5.C6T49   1990
   648.3′041—dc20   90-40664
                                                                             CIP

Copyright © 1991 by Sondra Thiederman

Published simultaneously in Canada
Printed in the United States of America
Casebound International Standard Book Number: 0-669-21930-4
Library of Congress Catalog Card Number: 90-40664

The paper used in this publication meets
the minimum requirements of American National Standard
for Information Sciences—Permanence of Paper
for Printed Library Materials, ANSI Z39.48-1984. ∞™

Year and number of this printing:

91 92 93 94 8 7 6 5 4 3 2 1

For my husband Tom—
there is such sweet harmony
in our diversity.

Contents

Figures and Tables

Figures

Tables

Preface and Acknowledgments

Hollywood High is my alma mater. In the early 1960s, our idea of diversity depended on what clubs a classmate joined or whether a student was a "brain," a "jock," or a member of the folk song society. Today the term *diversity* has taken on a far different meaning at this one-time enclave of homogeneity. Roughly 87 percent of the student body is now foreign born. The students come from fifty-nine countries and speak ninety different languages. This degree of cultural and language diversity may be extreme, but it symbolizes the remarkable demographic changes that are affecting the United States today.

For American corporations and American managers, these changes mean access to a large pool of enthusiastic workers whose culturally different points of view can only add to the creativity and problem-solving resources of every organization. They also mean challenges: in communicating across language and accent barriers, in developing and maintaining teamwork and harmony despite differing styles and values, and in learning to motivate in the face of diverse needs and expectations.

The issues raised by cultural diversity are not new to twentieth-century America. As far back as 1781, Thomas Jefferson wrote that immigrants would render the population of the nation a "heterogeneous, incoherent, distracted mass." Absurd though this comment is, the real irony lies in that President Jefferson composed it when 80 percent of the population was from the British Isles. I wonder how he would have felt about the more than 110 languages spoken in the nation today.

As we look around us, we see the result of Jefferson's "heterogeneous, incoherent, distracted mass." We see, as Walt Whitman said, "not merely a nation, but a nation of nations"—immigrants and their descendants who have learned to live together in harmony and who have pooled their diverse skills and values to build the foundation of American industry. The purpose of this book is to supply the management tools with which to perpetuate this tradition of harmony and growth.

Although this purpose is clear and the need obvious, it is not an easy task to write about cultural differences. The problem is that discussing the differences among cultures is tricky business; there are many pitfalls on the road to presenting the material clearly and fairly. One of the most frightening of these pitfalls is the constant danger of inadvertently offending someone because of a misunderstanding, faulty generality, or accidental misstatement of fact.

After more than ten years' experience as a speaker and trainer on the topic of cross-cultural communication, I naively assumed that I had long since figured out how to avoid these dangers. I thought that all I had to do was polish up my workshops, struggle with the word processor a bit, and, presto, a work of complete accuracy and infinite equity would appear.

I soon found, however, that there is something ominous about discussing so delicate a topic in print; there is no room for the last-minute aside to cover tracks, no way of reading the audience's reaction or responding to criticisms from the floor. When giving a presentation, I encourage the audience to disagree with me, to raise issues, to request elaboration, and to voice dissatisfaction. Unfortunately, readers do not have the same luxury of immediate rebuttal.

To compensate somewhat for this limitation, I ask you to bear in mind that although I have made every effort to present accurate information and to avoid faulty generalities or stereotypes, there is still the possibility that some comments may inadvertently disturb you. I extend my apologies for this and invite your patience. Human behavior is by no means an exact science; as all managers who work in a multicultural setting realize, it is changeable and, blessedly, inconsistent. It is in this inconsistency that the fascination of cultural diversity lies.

Acknowledgments

The content of this book was culled from a number of sources. Among these were the participants in dozens of cultural-awareness workshops, whose enthusiasm and willingness to share provided many valuable insights. Information about language diversity and material for appendix A was generously contributed by Elizabeth Mariscal and Krystyna Srutwa of SpeechCraft, and by Paco Sevilla, Elizabeth Estes, and my friend and colleague, Susan Montepio. Susan's insights into the complexities of Filipino culture were also indispensable. A special thank you must go to my dear friend, Molly Drummond, who lent both unbridled enthusiasm and exceptional proofreading skills to the project.

Every author thanks family, friends, teachers, and colleagues for their support. Perhaps this is because the one thing we all have in common, despite our cultural diversity, is the reliance on other people for love and inspiration.

The challenge of writing this book could not have been met without the foundation laid by my mother and father. My mother's enthusiasm for knowledge and my father's penchant for taking on the most difficult of tasks were contagious. The need to learn was nurtured by my high school history teacher—who was also our sometimes victorious football coach—Lou Birnbaum, and by Wayland Hand, my mentor and friend during the long graduate years at UCLA.

The support of family and friends too numerous to mention was a source of energy and warmth that formed an essential ingredient to the success of this project. Mom Thiederman, Jane, and Åke brought their diverse brands of love to the long struggle. My sister, Susan, and my many friends old and new, tolerated my lack of attention and, at times I am sure, very tiresome state of preoccupation. My daughter, Shea, and stepdaughter, Krista, showed an enthusiasm and support far beyond their years. And finally, my dear husband, Tom, to whom this book is dedicated, supplied the love and patience that made it all possible.

—Sondra Thiederman, Ph.D.
San Diego, California

Introduction

Immigration . . . the sincerest form of flattery.
—Anonymous

This book takes a straightforward look at the complex subject of cultural diversity. It is an easy-to-use guide that es-
corts readers through the often perplexing terrain of the
multicultural workplace. If you are seeking a theoretical discussion of the processes of cultural adaptation or the nature of
culture, or the dynamics of diversity, this book is not for you.

You have probably picked up this book for one of three
reasons:

1. You are a human-resource professional who wishes to
   help your managers and supervisors manage immigrant or
   ethnic workers more effectively.

2. You are a manager who wants to learn the skills and
   techniques necessary to improve productivity, harmony,
   and teamwork in the multicultural workplace.

3. You find yourself working around colleagues, employees,
   and superiors of diverse backgrounds and wish to understand this diversity better.

If you fall into one of these categories, this book will provide
you with both the general principles and practical techniques
with which to manage diversity more effectively.

Why Learn about Cross-Cultural Management?

The material in this book will allow you to maximize the
chances that your multicultural workplace will be productive,

efficient, and harmonious. It will also enable you to attract and retain high-quality workers of diverse ethnic or cultural backgrounds.

It will allow you to facilitate:

- Better communication despite accent and language barriers

- More effective motivation of workers through the accurate interpretation of behaviors and the design of culturally aware motivation strategies

- The accurate evaluation of culturally diverse applicants and employees through a better understanding of presentation styles, behaviors, and language facility

- Harmony and comfort in the workplace through an understanding of the motivations and perspectives of others

It will allow you to minimize:

- Worker alienation that can result from misunderstandings of etiquette, values, and behaviors

- Costly discrimination suits that arise from poor communication and worker alienation

- Unnecessary terminations that result from communication breakdown and misinterpretation of employee behavior

- Your managers' reluctance to hire and work with culturally diverse workers

- Racism and discrimination that can result from misinterpretations of the behaviors of others

If you are a human-resource professional who will teach cross-cultural management techniques to your managers, this book will supply not only content but training methods and suggestions on how to overcome trainees' resistance and expedite the learning process.

Who Is This Book About?

This book is about workers who bring to the workplace a culture and/or language different from that held by mainstream American society. These individuals may be immigrants or ethnic populations who, although born in the United States, still observe their cultural roots and speak their native language.

Although various ethnic groups are mentioned, those discussed most are Asians and Hispanics, the largest immigrant populations found in the United States today. This does not mean, of course, that the information supplied in this book is applicable only to these groups. Many of the techniques for effective communication and motivation apply to any cross-cultural relationship and are just as valuable when working with an Arab as when interacting with a Swede. For example, the technique of looking at the nonnative English speaker's lips in order to understand him or her better is applicable with any immigrant worker as is the importance of correctly pronouncing the names of all employees, no matter how unfamiliar those names might be.

Obviously if this book is about workers and about how to manage them, it is also about managers. You will notice that there are frequent references to mainstream American managers, American managers, or to an all-encompassing *us* or *we*. These labels in no way imply that the readers or the managers who will benefit from this book were all born and raised in the United States or that they are of white, Anglo-Saxon extraction. What it does imply, however, is that the manager who needs this material was either raised in the values and perspective of mainstream American culture or has become largely assimilated into that culture. The same distinction applies to any references to the mainstream American or American worker.

Many of your managers, and many who will read this book on their own, are either ethnic or foreign born but have adopted the methods of American management and the culture of mainstream American society. These managers, as well as the native born, will benefit from learning about other cultures and about the techniques necessary to communicate across cultural and language barriers.

What about the Problem of Generalities?

One of the cardinal sins when dealing with cultural diversity is the making of broad general statements about groups of people. This point is driven home in chapter 1 and amplified throughout the rest of the book. Nevertheless, the most casual of readers will notice that these pages are filled with general statements like, "Vietnamese workers are likely to feel uncomfortable drawing attention to themselves" or, "Mexican males prefer being addressed by their last names."

There is really no excuse for generalities such as these. On the other hand, it would be extremely cumbersome to stop at every statement to reiterate that it is a generality and does not pertain to all members of the group in question. Every statement in this book is intended as a guideline only. To apply any cultural characteristic to all individuals within a particular population would be unwise, and also disrespectful to the uniqueness of that human being.

Generalities become still more dangerous when large populations like Asians, Hispanics, or Middle Easterners are lumped together; "Middle Eastern males tend to stand close to you when conversing" is a good example. Certainly members of these groups share common cultural characteristics, but there is also considerable diversity. Puerto Ricans, for example, are very different from Cubans as are Laotians from Koreans.

I have made every effort to avoid general statements and to focus only on those characteristics that are common to the larger group. The importance of the community over the individual, for example, is widespread throughout Asia, although it is manifested somewhat differently in Japan than it is in China.

To take the problem of generalities one step further, sometimes I ascribe a characteristic or attitude to foreign-born or ethnic workers in general. At first glance, this may appear to be a gross grouping of people who are very different from each other in culture and outlook; however, I have tried to ascribe to these large and diverse groups only those characteristics they might reasonably be expected to share. Respect for authority, for instance, is valued by most immigrant populations and distinguishes them from many native-born or highly assimilated American workers who are generally more comfortable with the prospect of questioning superiors and with availing themselves of participative management programs.

How Can You Get the Most Out of This Book?

There are a number of ways to approach this book. The following six tips will help you decide which approach to take and will guarantee that you get the most out of your time and effort:

1. *Before reading any further, take a moment to write down what you want to gain from this book.* Is your priority to learn how to train managers in cross-cultural management? Are you interested in learning to motivate more effectively? Is language diversity your greatest concern? Do you wish to understand the more general themes of cross-cultural communication? By focusing your thoughts in this way, you will be better able to watch for, and benefit from, the material that is of greatest interest to you.

2. *Decide if you want to read the book from start to finish or focus on particular chapters or sections.* Although it would be preferable to read the book from front to back, chapter by chapter, the content has been organized in such a way that readers can benefit from a more selective approach. Should there be specific information that you are after, the appendixes and index will be helpful.

3. *Watch for important themes that are repeated throughout the book.* The importance of saving face, for example, is discussed under values, etiquette, and motivation. These common threads are the meat of the material. If a point keeps coming up in the text, that means that it also appears with considerable regularity in the multicultural workplace.

4. *Honor the small bits of specific information as much as the more general principles.* The general themes of cross-cultural communication—the importance of avoiding stereotypes and the value of communicating respect, for example—are naturally of great significance because they apply to all instances of multicultural interaction. These general principles are, however, only part of the picture. The tiny pieces of information can be just as important. Knowing, for example, when to shake hands or what questions to ask can have a profound impact on the success of professional contacts. These seemingly inconsequential choices can communicate the respect necessary to cement a good working relationship.

5. *Do the exercises.* The exercises serve two purposes: they allow you to learn the material more readily and are valuable tools for training your managers. If you intend to conduct such training, doing the exercises will show you how they function and how appropriate they are to the specific problems of your organization. The appendixes contain additional devices useful for training.

5. *Use the Supplementary Reading list.* The list is especially helpful if you wish to go into some specific area in greater depth. Although by no means definitive, it is a good guide to the wealth of materials on cultural diversity currently available in libraries or bookstores.

How Can You Stretch Your Cultural Comfort Zone?

You will enjoy reading this book, and, by the time you are finished, I believe you will have learned to enjoy, or at least feel comfortable in, the multicultural workplace. Being around and learning about cultural diversity is an adventure—an adventure because diversity means new ideas, new perspectives, and a high probability of the unexpected.

Adventures are opportunities for new discoveries. They can

also be fraught with anxiety and discomfort. Ralph Waldo Emerson once said, "Knowledge is the antidote to fear." The more we know, the less ignorance we have and the less anxiety and discomfort we experience. I hope that by the time you finish this book, you will have stretched your "cultural comfort zone" just a bit and begun to see that diversity is an adventure not to be missed.

1
Confronting the Challenge
The First Steps toward Bridging Cultural Barriers

We may have come over on different ships, but we're all in the same boat now.

—Whitney Young, Jr.

This chapter covers:

- The nature and impact of culture
- Dealing with culture shock
- The importance of acknowledging diversity
- Dispelling stereotypes
- Overcoming ethnocentrism
- The value of being yourself amid cultural diversity

Almost one-quarter of the population of the United States were immigrants or of immigrant parentage. The year was 1920, and Ellis Island in New York City seemed to be the place to be or at least the place to be from. The nation had just experienced one of the largest waves of immigration in its history, a wave that would forever change the texture of American society and the nature of American culture.

Three-quarters of a century later it has happened again. This time the port of entry is no longer Ellis Island but the runways of Los Angeles, Miami, San Francisco, and New York, along with the beaches of Florida and the borders of the Southwest. The immigrants too have changed, emigrating not from Europe but from Asia, the Hispanic countries, and from the Middle East.

Like their predecessors, these new arrivals will eventually contribute to that process of cultural change that one early writer described as "a constant reflex action whereby the native modifies the foreign as much as the foreign modifies the native."[1] Just as it took decades to assess the impact of earlier immigrants on American culture, it will take years before we will see the final results of this reflex action.

What is obvious now is that these immigrants and their descendants are having a dramatic effect on the demographics of the work force and the culture of the workplace. Our tried-and-true motivation strategies, communication techniques, and management styles are no long universally applicable. Clearly, if we are to make the most of the creativity and energy that a diverse work force can supply, there is much to be learned from the cultural differences that have rendered so many of our notions of effective management obsolete.

Defining Culture

Culture consists of the rules and expectations that come into play when two human beings interact. It is an agreed-upon set of rules for living that consists of components ranging from seemingly inconsequential edicts about how to address a letter or style one's hair to grand ideas about the origins of the universe or the nature of God. Some of the ingredients of culture are:

- Etiquette
- Values
- Language
- Traditions and customs
- Food, dress, and musical tastes
- Belief systems and world views

These categories are not distinct but tend to overlap and influence each other. The value many immigrant and ethnic groups place on respect for authority, for example, is directly responsible for the preferred etiquette of addressing superiors by their last names. The Arab belief in the will of God is closely tied to the high value placed on fatalism and, in turn, to the etiquette of not aggressively seeking promotions in the workplace.

Just as culture tells us how to behave, it also colors our interpretation of the behavior of others. Because mainstream Americans might associate a hearty handshake with strength and fortitude, they are likely to assume, incorrectly, that the more gentle grasp of the Asian is a sign of weakness or indecisiveness. We shall see in the discussion of ethnocentrism that such assumptions can create serious misunderstandings in the multi-cultural workplace.

What Is the Purpose of Culture?

Culture simplifies the everyday decisions of living. It tells us what style of clothes to wear, how to behave on a date, and what cheer to chant at a football game. It also helps us with the greater challenges of maintaining harmony in society, achieving spiritual peace, and structuring our governmental bodies.

Although cultural rules are only informally agreed upon, they have an amazing ability to dictate ideas and behavior. Without them, society would be in disarray. Have you ever wondered, for example, who decided that it is "polite" to say "thank you" after an exchange? Some cultures consider it rude to say "thank you" because it ends what ought to be an infinite flow of give and take. Why do we think it intrusive when a stranger sits next to us in an empty subway car? In many other countries, it would be regarded as an insult if the person sat elsewhere.

This is not to say that every tenet put forward by every culture is strictly adhered to. Some cultural precepts might be regarded as more ideal than real. Mainstream American culture, for example, theoretically places great value on equality between its citizens. Although this idea is treasured by the majority of society, it is not consistently practiced. Examples of the dichotomy between that which is held up as ideal and that which is actually practiced are found throughout the world and is one reason that learning about other cultures can be so complex.

What Kinds of Cultures Are There?

The focus of this book is on national and ethnic cultures. There are, however, other kinds of cultures to be found in the workplace. Cultures differ, for example, between regions within the United States. Who would deny that the cultural style and etiquette of the Northeast is different from the South and, certainly, from the West Coast?

Similarly corporations, occupations, vocations, as well as gender and age groups all have unique values, style, and etiquette that qualify them as true cultures. We are all part of at least one of these subcultures, and for this reason each of us is exceptionally experienced in conducting ourselves properly in cross-cultural relationships.

You have probably had the challenge of adjusting to the values of a new company after a job change. Maybe you had to get used to a more casual, egalitarian style or, alternatively, adjust your expectations when it became obvious that your new corporate culture called for adherence to strict rules and respect for a firm hierarchy of leadership.

Perhaps you took up a new hobby and had to learn the etiquette of the ski slopes, the jargon of golf, or the "accepted" way to dress on the tennis courts. Or maybe you have had the wrenching experience of moving from a small town to a city where you discovered it was no longer proper to look everyone in the eye and say "good morning" to strangers but where you suddenly found new acquaintances calling you by your first name.

If you have ever been through any of these experiences, you are already initiated into the world of cultural diversity. Each is an example of cultural adaptation and requires the ability to observe another way of acting and make the adjustments necessary in the new situation.

Distinguishing Culture from Personality

How can we distinguish culture from personality? How can managers tell when an immigrant or ethnic worker's behavior or attitude is a reflection of cultural differences or simply a function of the individual's way of acting?

Although there is no easy answer to this dilemma and sometimes the only tool at the manager's disposal is instinct, one technique can help: observation. Observe the attitudes and behaviors of other employees in the workplace who share the same or similar ethnic background as the worker in question. If the behavior at issue is found among other workers of the same group, it is fairly safe to assume that it is rooted in cultural differences. If, for example, a large number of Mexican employees are reluctant to tell management of problems on the job, you can probably assume that this behavior is the result of a cultural sanction and not just the shyness of a number of individual workers. If many members of a particular group tend to be chronically late, it is likely that it is because of a culturally specific attitude about punctuality rather than an individual's laziness, lack of understanding, or transportation problems.

As we shall see in chapter 5, the accurate interpretation of a worker's actions is the first step toward motivating behavior change and has a direct impact on the design of effective motivation strategies. An approach based on an individual's personality is likely to be very different from one that is in response to a culturally generated behavior.

Understanding Culture Shock

You have no doubt heard the term *culture shock* and such spin-off phrases as *future shock* and *technoshock*. Culture shock is a state of mind that occurs when people find themselves immersed in a strange culture. It happens for three reasons:

1. The individual's behaviors are not getting the response that he or she is accustomed to.

2. The person realizes that he or she no longer knows the cultural rules of the game and does not understand how to behave.

3. The individual no longer receives appropriate credit for achievements, skills, or ideas.

With respect to item 1, for example, Filipino or West Indian workers who go out of their way to say "good morning" unfailingly to the busy manager may be met with irritation rather than gratitude. This behavior comes from the high cultural value placed on courtesy and formal behavior toward superiors.

A good example of item 2 involves the immigrant who is repeatedly invited to have lunch with the boss. The worker is likely to feel out of step with this cultural convention because such behavior would be considered inappropriate in his or her homeland.

Positive reinforcement and credit for skills and expertise can be lacking, for example, because the worker is hesitant to speak up with ideas at meetings out of fear of using English incorrectly. The impression is left that the employee has nothing to contribute or is passive and uninterested in participating in problem-solving sessions. The result is a worker who does not receive the credit that his or her abilities deserve.

Exercise 1–1 will help you and your managers better understand how culture shock feels. The questions in it are intended

---

Exercise 1–1. Experiencing Culture Shock

1. When I do something nice for someone and he or she becomes angry with me because of it, I feel . . .

2. When someone says something that I don't understand, I feel . . .

3. When something I say is misunderstood and everyone laughs, I feel . . .

4. When I want to shake hands with someone and he or she hugs me instead, I feel . . .

5. When I smile at someone who does not smile back, I feel . . .

---

to elicit the same emotions that members of your multicultural work force often feel. As you respond to each question, be candid and quick and resist the temptation to overanalyze your answers.

Probably some of your responses will include feelings of foolishness, inadequacy, embarrassment, disappointment, disorientation, and even anger. These are precisely the emotions that culturally different workers feel who are thrust, without previous orientation, into the American workplace.

How Does Culture Shock Affect the Workplace?

One certain effect of culture shock on the workplace is that it diminishes productivity. It is not just an abstract concept that makes people unhappy; it is a phenomenon that must be dealt with if efficiency and harmony are to be maintained.

Culture shock disrupts productivity because it produces mental states and behaviors that interfere with good work habits and peak performance. Among these are:

Depression   Loneliness

Aggression   The temptation to
                                   feign understanding

Short attention span   Passivity

Irritability   Quickness to fatigue

Frustration   Paranoia

Desire to avoid contact   Sensitivity to body
    with others   language

Feelings of inadequacy

The effect of most of these states on productivity is obvious, but a few warrant some discussion: feelings of inadequacy, loneliness, and feelings of aggression, frustration, and paranoia.

Feelings of inadequacy have a profound effect on any worker's willingness to attempt new and challenging tasks. These feelings are amplified among cultures in which saving face is a paramount value. For such workers, to attempt a new task, to raise an idea in a meeting, or to volunteer for a difficult project is to risk a humiliating failure. In cases like these, culture shock becomes part of a cycle. The employee's fear of voicing ideas or attempting new tasks results in a lack of credit for his or her natural abilities, which leads to further feelings of inadequacy, and the cycle continues.

Loneliness can have adverse effects by causing the immigrant worker to associate exclusively with others from the same country in the workplace in an effort to relieve the feelings of isolation. This behavior, known as clustering, can create resentment among other members of the work force. Care needs to be taken to diffuse this resentment because it can lead to diminished teamwork and increased conflict.

Particular sensitivity should also be shown toward feelings of aggression, frustration, and paranoia, which contribute to a disruptive atmosphere. Conflicts that might at first glance appear to be rooted in racism and prejudice are often caused instead by negative emotions, which arise naturally from feelings of disorientation, inadequacy, and culture shock.

When Does Culture Shock Strike?

A common misconception about culture shock is that it sets in immediately upon the immigrant's arrival in this country and dissipates as soon as he or she settles into a routine. Although sometimes culture shock does strike this quickly, it can take as long as two years to appear.

The reason for this delayed reaction is that when people first enter a new culture, their initial contacts with it are fairly super-ficial. Confusion over how public transportation works or how to find housing might be disturbing but does not affect the individual's confidence and self-esteem. Also, if family members and friends are here to greet new arrivals, the impact of their transition may be buffered until they find themselves in the working world.

After several months, however, the immigrant begins to un-derstand that his or her new culture is different on a deep level and that there is a great deal more adjusting to do than was at first realized. Getting along with people, for example, is not just a matter of smiling and being pleasant. The culture begins to demand more subtleties of behavior and more behaviors that run against the cultural grain of the immigrant and his or her fam-ily. This is why when we travel internationally for a vacation or even go for a few months sojourn in an overseas position, we may feel a bit confused, but rarely do the deep symp-toms of culture shock—depression and anger, for instance—appear.

Another complexity about culture shock is that it is likely to strike not only immigrant workers but also managers in a cul-turally diverse workplace. This happens because American managers have largely been taught to manage according to one set of rules and principles—a set that applies to largely white mainstream American workers who more or less share the same culture and have the same ideas regarding the work environment. The manager may, for example, find that tra-ditional measures like motivating by means of promotions or public praise do not work in the multicultural workplace. Such basic ideas as participative management may fall flat when pro-posed to workers raised in a more authoritarian atmosphere.

Managers are not immune to the emotions listed, and it is not unusual for them to begin to feel inadequate, frustrated, paranoid, and angry as they become more and more confused and culture shocked.

The problem for the cross-cultural trainer and the human-resource professional is that these emotions leave the manager resistant to learning new ways. Some managers tend to feel, understandably, that they have spent years learning to manage homogeneity and, just as it seems to be coming together, are being asked to learn a new game. Chapter 6, which discusses techniques for teaching this "new game," presents a number of methods for diffusing these negative feelings and breaking through the manager's resistance.

Another unfortunate effect of the manager's culture shock is a reluctance to hire diverse workers. Managers come to feel that if the number of culturally different workers can be kept to a minimum, the confusion and feelings of inadequacy will disappear. Fortunately, the opposite is closer to the truth. The more managers are exposed to diversity and the more experiences they have with different workers, the more comfortable and less "shocked" they will become.

How Can We Heal Culture Shock?

What can be done about culture shock? Exposure and education are important first steps. For both managers and workers, the more contact each has with the other's culture, the less disoriented both parties will feel.

Training too can be helpful. This means training for the manager to learn about the specifics of other cultures and about the skills of cross-cultural management. It also means training for the immigrant and, in some cases, the ethnic worker to become familiar with both the basics of mainstream American culture and the expectations of American management.

Another cure for culture shock is to bring the subject out in the open, admitting that it exists. Negative emotions always lose their punch once they are explained and understood. By pointing out what culture shock is, why it happens, and how it affects workers and managers alike, the "shock" quickly loses some of its intensity.

Acknowledging the Differences: The First Step toward Understanding

The person who said, "We do not have to be twins to be brothers" must have been well versed in the science of cultural diversity. This wise observer understood that it is all right, and even desirable, to notice the differences among peoples. It might even have been the same cultural philosopher who commented, "Just because we are equal does not mean we are the same."

It is permissible—and not racist—to acknowledge the differences among peoples and among cultures. The problem is that some of us are culture blind; we have difficulty seeing and recognizing cultural differences. People who are afflicted with culture blindness believe that the only thing that distinguishes nationalities is the language they speak. Besides language, the thinking goes, human beings are all alike.

If the culture blind of the world are correct and language is the only thing that separates us—if there are no true cultural differences among people—then why is it that there is such an adjustment when the assertive and direct New Yorker moves to the genteel South or the unwary American inadvertently offends a more staid and formal English colleague? Clearly there is a lot more to differences among peoples than just language.

Why Are We Reluctant to Notice Differences?

What is it about acknowledging cultural differences that makes people uncomfortable? Why do so many professionals today seem fond of saying that there is no cultural diversity in a given workplace even though it is populated by employees who were born and raised in many different environments?

The first reason for this reluctance is the delusion that if we notice the differences among peoples, we will be guilty of racism. In fact, it can be argued that the opposite is true. Ask yourself this question: If all cultures are alike, who are they like? What culture represents the norm to which they all conform?

The answer is easy. If all cultures are alike, they must be just like the culture of the observer—of our culture-blind American. What this amounts to is the negation of the unique characteristics, strengths, and weaknesses of any other group. It is a way of saying that the uniqueness of other cultures does not exist; "everybody is exactly alike, that is, like me."

We will look in a moment at the negative ramifications of this type of thinking. For now, let us just say that this attitude is disrespectful of ethnic or immigrant workers because it negates so much of who they are and ignores so many of their most cherished values and ways of acting.

We do not pretend that all our friends are exactly alike. Some enjoy the beach, and others are fond of football, or antique auctions, or social gatherings. If we ignore these differences, not only are we in danger of treating each friend inappropriately but we also fail to get the most out of the relationship. The same principle applies to the multicultural work force. Acknowledging and learning about the differences between cultures can only strengthen our relationships with the worker whose background is different from our own.

The second reason that people are reluctant to notice differences is the fear that if we look at how cultures differ, we will fail to see how they are alike. The reassuring fact is that human beings are more alike than they are different. We all have, for example, the same basic needs for dignity, survival, and social contact. What is different between groups is the way in which these needs are satisfied. The mainstream American, for example, achieves dignity through public accolades; an Asian would satisfy the same need through quiet contributions to the good of the community.

Another reason for this hesitance to see the difference among cultures is the concern that if we examine the ways in which people are different, we will automatically perpetuate stereotypes. This fear too is unfounded. Acknowledging that Germans use more formal titles or that Middle Easterners feel it is wrong to plan inordinately for the future are simple statements that need no more perpetuate stereotypes than if we were to acknowledge that southern Californians tend to be health-conscious, human-resource professionals good with people or that southerners tend to be hospitable.

Obviously these statements do not apply to every southern Californian, human-resource professional, or southerner; they are merely general guidelines. But just because they are not universally true is no reason to avoid the subject altogether. In the discussion of stereotypes to follow, we will examine ways to distinguish between informative guidelines about cultural groups and confining stereotypes that interfere with understanding.

Simple denial is the fourth reason that so many of us do not want to notice differences. Life is easier, though a great deal less interesting, if we assume that everyone is alike. This way of thinking eliminates all fear of making a mistake, all need to learn new ways, and all necessity to make uncomfortable adjustments. To notice differences is to open up a world of complexity and uncertainly that can create feelings of inadequacy and culture shock. Many people would just as soon avoid facing these challenges.

Finally, when we have the courage to notice the differences among people, we are forced to face the fact that our own culture does not have a monopoly on truth. It raises the prospect that we can learn from other cultures and that our way may not be the only way. To some this realization is exciting; to others it is a threat that makes the acknowledgment of cultural differences an intimidating prospect.

Why Is It Important to Notice Differences?

If it is true, as Ralph Waldo Emerson said, that "fear springs from ignorance," then ignoring the differences among cultures can only perpetuate the discomfort found in the multicultural workplace. This is the first reason that it is important to acknowledge diversity.

The more we know about something, the more control we will feel and the less disorientation or culture shock will be experienced. By noticing and learning about other cultures, managers will become more comfortable with diversity and therefore more willing to hire, work with, and promote the culturally different worker.

Another reason to acknowledge differences is that to do so

communicates respect for the worker's culture. The importance of communicating respect cannot be overemphasized. It is one of the basic principles of successful cross-cultural communication and management. When we disregard the unique characteristics of someone's culture, we are negating an important part of that person's identity. Mexicans, for example, place great value on the development of well-rounded relationships. Once the manager realizes this, he or she can communicate respect for that value and, in turn, for the Mexican worker, by taking time to chat and learn more about that individual. Small gestures like this can have far-reaching effects in terms of generating reciprocal respect and increased cooperation.

Finally, and for purposes of this book perhaps most important, is the fact that only by noticing the unique values, expectations, and desires of immigrant and ethnic workers will managers be able to motivate and communicate effectively. Although numerous examples of this fact are found in chapter 5 where we examine the importance of honoring culturally specific needs, one instance here will serve to illustrate the point. According to mainstream American culture, rolling up one's sleeves and working beside subordinates is a sign of an egalitarian attitude bound to motivate increased teamwork and respect. Many Asian workers, however, interpret this same behavior as an insult and an implication that the employee's work is lacking. In extreme cases, such an insult, and the accompanying loss of face, could result in the Asian's resignation. Also, the worker might lose respect for the manager who would have been expected to remain more aloof.

The practical ramifications of ignoring differences such as these are obvious. If we do not notice, learn about, and respond to cultural diversity, miscalculations will be made that can easily compromise the efficiency, harmony, and productivity of the workplace.

Identifying and Avoiding Stereotypes

Have you ever noticed that when you do not know very much about a category of things, everything within that category looks alike? Sailboats are an example. There are dozens of different kinds of sailboats, each with a unique design and function and each with different strengths and weaknesses. When most of us look out into a harbor, however, all we see are dozens of boats floating on the water; they all look alike to landlubbers.

For a true sailor, on the other hand, or even the dedicated hobbyist, no two sailboats are exactly alike. Some are faster, some sturdier, some meant for long journeys across the sea, and others for leisurely cruises up the coast. The difference between the casual observer and the devoted sailor is knowledge. As we learn more about sailboats, each vessel begins to look unique, and the stereotype that "all sailboats are just pretty white things that float on the water" begins to fade.

The same applies to knowledge about cultures. The more we know about a particular group, the less likely we are to lump the individuals together and say that they are all alike.

When we say *stereotype*, what are we talking about? The term *stereotype* is a bit of industry jargon that originated in the world of printing. A stereotype was an inflexible mold used to print the same image over and over again. For our purposes, the word refers to inflexible statements about a category of people. Stereotypical statements are applied to all members of a group without regard for individual differences.

A stereotype is by no means the same as information about another culture. It is possible to say, for example, that Middle Eastern men tend to maintain direct eye contact or that Greeks generally place great value on personal honor, without being guilty of stereotyping.

The distinction is that stereotypical statements are inflexible. Stereotypes assume that everyone from a group has certain characteristics and allow no room for individual differences. General facts about a group, like those presented in this book, are merely guidelines or starting points. To say, for example, that Laotians tend to be good at repetitive tasks or that Asians on the whole value education is merely to present guidelines—bits of information that certainly do not apply to everyone.

Stereotypes can be positive as well as negative, but both types are equally distorting and destructive. Two stereotypes, for example, that have been responsible for a great deal of injustice in the United States are that African-Americans are musical and athletic. These are wonderful talents, but to apply them to every member of the group serves only to confine all African-Americans to these categories of achievement.

Why Do We Stereotype?

The primary reason that people stereotype is to relieve anxiety. It is human nature to feel anxious when situations are ambiguous or behavior is unpredictable. By stereotyping, by constructing categories and boxes into which human beings can be placed, this anxiety is relieved, and we regain a sense of control and predictability.

Although stereotypical thinking is certainly not confined to the United States, it is a practice that fits well with the American character and the nature of mainstream American culture. Americans tend to be linear in their thinking, rational, and attuned to consistent cause-and-effect relationships. Situations and behaviors that are ambiguous and not neatly pigeonholed are difficult for many Americans to tolerate.

We have what psychologists call a "confirmation bias"—a desire to fit new information into old categories. What this means for our relationships with culturally diverse workers and colleagues is that if someone does not fit our stereotype of what people in that category are like, we will distort our perception of the external reality to fit our expectations.

Let us look at the case of Martha, a human-resource director at a large hotel in California.

> Martha had a sales position to fill and needed someone who was very outgoing, talkative, and assertive. One of the applicants for the job was a young woman named Katsumi who was born and raised in Japan.
>
> During the interview, Katsumi was extremely gregarious and outgoing; she did not fit the usual stereotype of Japanese women as shy, unassertive, and retiring. Because Martha had internalized the stereotype of the soft-spoken Japanese woman, she could not accept that Katsumi was

really suited to the sales position. In order to reconcile her previous idea of Japanese women with the extroverted applicant in her office, Martha rationalized that Katsumi was merely nervous during the interview and was not ordinarily so talkative.

Martha's refusal to see what was in front of her eyes, to abandon her stereotypical thinking, caused her to make a serious mistake. Rather than place Katsumi in the sales position for which she was obviously highly qualified, Martha applied another stereotype and assumed that "all Asian women are good at math." She arranged for a position for Katsumi in the accounting department, where she proceeded to do a very poor job.

Before long, reports filtered up to Martha's office that although Katsumi was not very good with numbers, she certainly had a lovely, outgoing personality and was particularly charming on the telephone. Fortunately, Martha had the courage and wisdom to admit her mistake and promptly transferred the young woman to the sales department.

Certainly there are times when individuals do fit the stereotypes that we hold. After all, stereotypes originated somewhere. The problem is that when our stereotypes are confirmed, we take this as evidence that we were right all along. When someone does not fit our stereotype, as in the case of Katsumi, we ignore it; when the person conforms to our previous idea, we give this evidence far more weight than it deserves.

Why Are Stereotypes Often Inaccurate?

Individual members of a culture differ for a variety of reasons. Socioeconomic status, for example, can account for considerable diversity within a given culture. It is, in fact, variations in education level, social strata, and financial status that account for most of the differences that exist among members of a particular group.

Further, individuals from various regions within one nation

may vary as dramatically as midwesterners from Californians. Mexicans from rural areas have a style very different from those from the more urbane neighborhoods of Mexico City. And Filipinos from Manila speak a different dialect and have a culture that varies significantly from that of Filipinos scattered throughout the Philippine Islands.

Older members of a group might adhere to their native culture more closely than do more youthful immigrants and men are likely to manifest a culture differently from women. Hispanic and Middle Eastern males, for example, are generally more assertive and direct than their female counterparts.

The validity of any stereotype is compromised by the amount of time that the worker has been in the United States and the degree of assimilation that has taken place. After an immigrant has been in the United States for some time, it becomes very difficult to predict just how much of his or her original culture is still being adhered to.

The historical experiences of individuals can also make it difficult to generalize about cultural features. The reasons for different workers' migration to the United States, for example, can vary and can have a tremendous impact on each person's perspective and values. The Vietnamese, Cuban, or Iranian who has come here as a matter of survival may have a very different attitude from the Korean who has come, in the old tradition, to seek the American dream.

Individual psychology must also be considered. We all know people who appear to conform to the ideals of mainstream American culture. When we get to know them better, however, it becomes obvious that their outlook is far more consistent with the culture of Great Britain, Japan, or Scandinavia. Their personality just does not fit with mainstream American values, and to treat them as if it does is to be disrespectful and to make some grave errors in judgment. The same applies to people from other cultures. Some individuals do not fit, in terms of style or temperament, into the stereotypical mold of the culture of which they are a part.

Finally, and much to the dismay of the already confused manager, it is impossible to predict the behavior of one person over time. Just as members of a cultural group are not all alike, each individual can change under different circumstances. No matter how well a worker may fit into a national or ethnic stereotype, outside events can cause his or her behavior to vary. In times of crises, for example, or when under pressure, even the most assimilated immigrant worker may suddenly revert to his or her culturally specific way of dealing with the situation. This happens because the process of assimilation usually takes place from the outside in—behaviors change first, with the attitudes that underlie those behaviors changing last.

When a crisis strikes, as when there is extreme stress on the job, these underlying attitudes can emerge and abruptly begin to affect behaviors. Immigrant workers who have completely bought into American values may even surprise themselves when, in times of crises, they begin to call upon long-forgotten culturally specific coping mechanisms. The Laotian who goes to the ethnic community for help, the Japanese who quits because of loss of face, or the Mexican who turns to the group leader for representation are all examples of how cultural roots can affect behavior years after the process of assimilation is apparently complete.

Why Are Stereotypes Dangerous?

All Mexicans are family loving; all Japanese are technically skilled; all French are good cooks; all Germans are efficient. Each of these is a "positive" stereotype, and yet each is just as destructive and dangerous as the most vile racial slur. The reason is that positive stereotypes limit our definition of a person.

You might say that stereotypes result in cases of mistaken identity. They interfere with our ability to see people for who they really are, they negate the individual, and they minimize the likelihood that workers will be valued for the traits and skills that they, as individuals, truly possess.

We have already seen how human-resource professionals and managers such as Martha can make faulty hiring decisions and inappropriate assignments because of stereotypical thinking. Another example might be the Hispanic male who has applied for a department change but has been turned down because it meant working with a female supervisor. The manager assumed that because of the applicant's cultural heritage, he would be uncomfortable working under a female.

In both cases, the manager made assumptions about the worker's personality, skill, and cultural background. This sort of prejudgment results in losses for all concerned. Not only does management lose out on many fine workers, but employees miss the opportunity of working in positions where their unique talents can be demonstrated. Asians, for example, tend to be passed over for management positions because of the stereotypical belief that they lack management ability, are not authoritarian enough, and have poor communication skills.

Stereotypes *can* be self-fulfilling. When we assume because of prejudgments that workers are incapable of something, we fail to give them the opportunity either to prove themselves or to learn the skill. This, in turn, perpetuates the stereotype and continues the cycle of prejudgments and inaccurate conclusions.

How Can We Eliminate Stereotypes?

The first step in eliminating stereotypical thinking is to become aware of the stereotypes that each of us carries with us. The idea is to separate our genuine knowledge about particular groups from those inflexible notions that have become lodged in our brains because of past experiences, rumor, or media influences.

Exercise 1–2 is designed to facilitate this process. The instructions are simple. After the name of each group, write down those characteristics that come to mind immediately. Do not stop to think too much about your response, and do not try to be fair, reasonable, or rational. What we are after here is an immediate emotional reaction. No one will ever see the list; you need not worry about appearing racist or prejudicial.

After you write your responses, jot down the source of your information. Was it a childhood experience, an incident in your working environment, television, the movies, or something your parents used to say? Again, do not edit your reply. Be spontaneous and, above all, be honest.

Exercise 1–2. Stereotype Awareness

	Your First Response	Source
Hispanics		
Filipinos		
Southeast Asians		
Blacks/African Americans		
Middle Easterners		
Mainstream Anglo-Americans		

You probably noticed a couple of interesting things about this exercise. First, if you are of Anglo extraction, you may have had trouble thinking of a quick response to the "mainstream

Anglo-American" category. The reason for this difficulty brings us back to the importance of learning about groups in order to diffuse stereotypes. You obviously know a great deal about Anglo-American culture and are also acquainted with many different types of Anglo-Americans. Add to this the fact that, in some ways, you yourself do not conform to the prevailing stereotypes, and you are left with the knowledge that blanket statements simply do not apply.

Probably, too, the sources for the characteristics that you listed were quite feeble. Did you formulate your ideas about Hispanics from television or the movies? Has the evening news dictated your image of the Middle East, and did the news footage of the Vietnam War leave you with an impression of the Vietnamese as weak and downtrodden? Perhaps one or two experiences with African-Americans dictated your first response to that group.

Do not feel bad if this is what shows up on your test. It is just human nature. The point here is to learn to distinguish our inflexible stereotypes from well-founded, flexible information about a group. Once we are able to identify our stereotypes for what they are, it is not difficult to set them aside. Of course, they will still pop into your mind when you see a Hispanic surname or an Asian face, but the goal is that you will be able to recognize them, shove them aside, and see that individual worker for who he or she really is.

Another means of diffusing stereotypes is to have multiple experiences with and in-depth knowledge of particular groups. We saw that our familiarity with Anglo-Americans made it difficult to stereotype. The same process applies to any group with whom you have extensive contact.

The more you learn about groups, the less able you will be to lump individuals together. The Frenchman Michel de Montaigne said in the sixteenth century, "Nothing is so firmly believed as that which we least know." Acquiring knowledge can only weaken stereotypical thinking. It is ignorance and lack of familiarity that makes all those sailboats look alike.

Ethnocentrism: Knowing Ourselves in Order to Know Others

The term *ethnocentrism* has many connotations. It carries with it implications of racial superiority, cultural elitism, and the insinuation that other cultures are exactly like ours or, if they are not, they ought to be.

For purposes of this discussion, ethnocentrism means that human beings tend to assume that the behaviors of others, no matter what their origins, can be interpreted according to the rules and values of one's own culture. It is as if our culture is the pivotal way of life toward which everyone else is striving.

The corollary of this perspective is that all people behave the way they do for identical reasons—that everybody's actions have the same meaning and arise from identical motivations. Psychologists call this a *self-reference criterion*—the unconscious process by which we evaluate everything according to that which we already know.

This simply is not true. Identical actions can have very different meanings in the context of various cultures. Nonetheless, ethnocentrism is part of the human condition. It is as if at birth we all don a pair of culturally tinted glasses through which we view and interpret the events of the world.

Ruth Benedict, an anthropologist, put it well when she said, "No man ever looks at the world with primitive eyes. He sees it edited by a definite set of customs and institutions and ways of thinking."[2] Benedict's customs, institutions, and ways of thinking are the pigments used to tint our cultural glasses.

Why Is Ethnocentrism a Problem?

There is nothing wrong with liking and even preferring one's own culture. The difficulty arises when we allow that culture to distort what we see. For managers, this distortion often takes the form of misinterpreting the meaning behind the culturally different worker's behavior.

Such misinterpretations can cause serious problems in the

workplace. Assume, for example, that you have called a Cambodian woman into your office to discuss a problem with her work. As you begin to speak, she drops her eyes and keeps them averted during the entire conversation. Naturally you will have a reaction to this behavior and will draw some assumptions about its meaning. This is especially true because it is a behavior to which you are probably unaccustomed. The important question is: What information will you use when figuring out why your worker averted her eyes? Most likely, you will call upon that knowledge most readily available to you: your own cultural assumptions about what lack of eye contact means.

In American culture, people who avoid eye contact are thought to be dishonest, shy, uninterested in what is being said, distracted, or guilty of something. If the worker with the wandering eye was raised in or assimilated into mainstream American culture, these might be fairly accurate assumptions. But our Cambodian worker grew up in an environment that taught a very different set of rules. Cambodian culture dictates that to look someone, particularly a superior, directly in the eye is to be rude, intrusive, and disrespectful. By looking away, this employee is communicating respect and deference to her boss; she believes she is behaving properly for an employee. This is just one example of how projecting the rules and expectations of one's own culture onto someone else can interfere with the all-important step of interpreting his or her behavior correctly.

Cultural projection is not a one-way process. Just as native-born Americans can be ethnocentric toward culturally different workers, immigrant employees can also project their own rules of behavior and motivation onto colleagues and managers. When American managers ask foreign-born workers for their opinions about a project, the workers are likely to interpret this action as a sign of weakness and indecisiveness. This interpretation may seem strange to American-born colleagues but becomes logical when we remember that many immigrant workers were raised in cultures in which managers are more authoritarian and rarely, if ever, ask the advice of workers.

In asking for suggestions, the manager is attempting to empower the workers, promote teamwork, and practice participative management. Unless these intentions are clearly spelled out, the message could be lost on the immigrant worker and the manager's good intentions thwarted.

Another example of cultural misunderstanding involves the fact that Americans, especially in certain parts of the country, tend to form friendships quickly and to speak relatively openly of intimate matters and feelings. To other native-born or assimilated Americans, this attitude is a sign of warmth and compassion. To workers from cultures in which relationships are cultivated more slowly but in which friendships last a lifetime, such behavior might be interpreted as intrusive, frivolous, and even rude. Both managers and workers need to learn about each other's culture in order to avoid the misunderstandings that ethnocentrism can create.

Why Do We Cling to Ethnocentrism?

Knowing that an ethnocentric attitude can create problems and distortions does not usually stop us from projecting our cultures onto other people. This is because it is comforting to believe that all behaviors, regardless of where they originate, can be understood according to the values that are so familiar and that we, in most cases, respect and cherish.

If we accept the fact that this is not the case, that we no longer have the luxury of looking at the world through our culturally tinted glasses, it means that we have more to learn. It also means that we must admit that our old ways do not necessarily work effectively in a culturally diverse environment.

Overcoming Ethnocentrism I: Why Learn about Others?

There are two steps to overcoming ethnocentrism. You are in the process of accomplishing one of these right now: you are learning about different cultures. This is not to say that it is necessary to become an anthropologist in order to solve the problem of ethnocentrism or that you will be able to learn all the specific behaviors that characterize various cultures. What you will be able to learn, however, are some of the cultural values and patterns that lie behind and motivate those behaviors. For example, it is more important to know about the value many foreign-born workers place on respect for authority than to memorize the details of how that respect is manifested. Once you have the general principle in hand, it is a relatively easy matter to apply it to the behaviors you see. A little knowledge will give you the insights necessary to substitute the correct, culturally aware interpretation for the old habit of projecting your own culture onto the situation.

You will be better able to understand why a Laotian worker might not take the initiative on tasks or why the Salvadoran may refrain from taking issue with the trainer. Awareness of the culturally rooted desire not to offend or question the manager or trainer will prevent you from taking the ethnocentric perspective that these workers are lazy, lacking in confidence, or uninterested in learning.

Overcoming Ethnocentrism II: Why Learn about Ourselves?

The second step to overcoming ethnocentrism is to become aware of those culturally tinted glasses that distort perception and cause us to misinterpret the behaviors of others. This does not mean that the glasses need to be removed but merely that we must know they are there so that we can compensate for the distortions they create.

Sunglasses make the world look dark and cloudy. Because we know we have them on, however, we are aware that it is not going to rain; we know that the cloudiness is an illusion created by the glasses. Because of this awareness, we do not react to the apparent overcast by running back in the house to retrieve an umbrella. On the other hand, if we did not know that our glasses were tinted, we could easily make that misjudgment and react inappropriately.

Knowing that you are wearing sunglasses may be no great challenge, but becoming conscious of your culture is not so easy. To paraphrase Ruth Benedict, "It is hard to become aware of the eyes through which we see."[3] Culture has been a part of us since the day we were born; it is in the makeup of our personalities, and it surrounds us like the air we breathe. We simply do not see it.

There are a number of techniques and exercises that can help you and your managers facilitate this difficult process of cultural self-awareness. Each is designed to make you conscious of your own culturally specific points of view. The goal is similar to that we have already accomplished with respect to stereotypes: to become aware of them so that they can be prevented from distorting your perception of particular groups.

One of the complexities in becoming culturally self-aware is that everyone has a number of cultures to get to know. National origin is only one of many categories of culture. We know that there are occupational cultures, regional or even neighborhood cultures, the culture of males and females, and cultures associated with hobbies and avocations. Just about any group designation you can think of shares some values, etiquette, rules of behavior, and an agreed-upon set of rules for living that constitute a culture.

Exercise 1–3 will help you become aware of those cultures that are part of your life and that you are likely to project unconsciously onto other people. The idea behind this exercise is for you and your managers to write down three cultures that influence your behavior and then enter three characteristics of those cultures. The cultures you pick might be from any of the categories that have been mentioned, ranging from mainstream American culture to the rituals of your bridge club. The characteristics might be values, rituals, customs, etiquette, jargon, or any other cultural feature you can think of. One entry has been filled in to get you started.

Probably one of the cultures that many of you list will be the American culture. There are those who would argue that there is no such thing as "American culture." Even Mark Twain commented that the only thing Americans have in common as a culture is a "fondness for ice water."

People talk about the "melting pot" and say that the United States is nothing but a conglomeration of cultures from around

Exercise 1–3. Cultural Self-Awareness

Culture: Southern California

Characteristics:

1. like the outdoors
2. informal
3. enjoy automobiles

Culture:

Characteristics:

1.
2.
3.

Culture:

Characteristics:

1.
2.
3.

Culture:

Characteristics:

1.
2.
3.

the world. This may be true, but it is from that very fabric that American culture grew—from the Puritan work ethic brought by the English to the "all-American" German hot dog, and such "American" French words as *rendezvous* and *hors d'oeuvres*.

Some rather strange comments have been made about American culture, many of them by foreigners. The Frenchman Alexis de Tocqueville, for example, commented that he knew "of no country, indeed, where the love of money has taken a stronger hold on the affections of man." A century and a half later, the Duke of Windsor was equally disparaging about a completely different aspect of American culture. His comment was that the thing that impressed him most about American society was the way the parents obeyed the children. At least Oscar Wilde seemed somewhat ambivalent about our way of life. He described America as a land of "unmatched vitality and vulgarity" and Americans as "a people who care not at all about values other than their own, and who, when they make up their minds, love you and hate you with a passionate zeal."

Colorful as these comments are, there is obviously a great deal more to our culture than obedient parents or the love of money. Exercise 1–4 is a starting point in understanding American culture and in becoming aware of the values that color, and sometimes distort, our perceptions. Proverbs are said to embody the essence of a culture. Some of the aphorisms listed in the box may seem antiquated and quaint, but they represent the central tenets upon which American society is built. Look at them, and write down the value that each saying represents.

The details of American culture will be discussed in appropriate sections throughout the book, but a quick look at the values reflected in each of the proverbs in exercise 1–4 (page 30) can serve as a starting point.

The first proverb, "There's no fool like an old fool," illustrates the value placed on youth in our nation. This perspective is in sharp contrast with the way in which other cultures respect and honor the elderly.

"God helps those who help themselves" along with idioms like "stand on your own two feet," emphasizes the importance

Exercise 1–4. Proverbs on "The American Way"

Proverb	Value
There's no fool like an old fool.	
God helps those who help themselves.	
The early bird catches the worm.	
A rolling stone gathers no moss.	
Take the bull by the horns.	
The sweetest grapes hang the highest.	
If at first you don't succeed, try, try again.	
There's more than one way to skin a cat.	
A stitch in time saves nine.	
Busy hands are happy hands.	

of independence of the individual. Again, this contrasts with the value many immigrant and ethnic families place on loyalty to and reliance on the extended family. This same proverb also illustrates the American belief in our ability and obligation to take control of our lives, a view that differs from that held by such cultures as the Filipino and Thai in which major life changes such as promotions and job transfers are best left up to fate.

"The early bird catches the worm" connotes both productivity and punctuality—the importance of getting work done and doing it promptly. "Never put off 'til tomorrow what you can do today" supports this idea of the efficient use of time.

"A rolling stone gathers no moss," along with many other aphorisms such as "don't let the grass grow under your feet," points to a preoccupation with horizontal and vertical mobility and speed. This differs from the perspective of the immigrant worker who recognizes the benefits of putting down roots and staying in one home, company, and occupation for a long time. These workers are not always anxious to seek a promotion or move to another firm.

Curiously, the Japanese have a proverb that is almost identical to this one, but in their case it is an injunction against mobility, not a praise of it. For the Japanese, the moss symbolizes valued traditions. The idea is that if the individual is in constant motion and does not stop long enough to acquire tradition and custom, he or she will have missed something of great importance in life.

"Take the bull by the horns" continues the theme of assertiveness and action, and "The sweetest grapes hang the highest" connotes that striving for the top should always be the priority. This latter proverb might also be interpreted to mean that "the grass is always greener on the other side of the hill"—another way of stating the American desire for constant progress and movement. "If at first you don't succeed, try, try again" promotes the idea of perseverance, as do other proverbs such as "you can't keep a good man down."

"There's more than one way to skin a cat" is a call not only for perseverance but for creativity and ingenuity as well. Creativity is, of course, a universal human trait, but not everyone considers it appropriate in the workplace. Some immigrant cultures feel that once a task is learned, changing the way in which it is performed is inappropriate and unwise. For this reason, it can sometimes take considerable persuasion to retrain workers who have become accustomed to doing a procedure in a particular way.

"A stitch in times saves nine" suggests the inclination for native-born and assimilated Americans to plan for the future. This trait distinguishes the United States from many other cultures where the emphasis is on living in the present moment with dignity and honor. In the world of human resources, this attitude is seen in the hesitation of some immigrant workers to contribute to retirement funds or to accumulate sick days.

"Busy hands are happy hands," along with the more antique saying, "Idle hands are the devil's workshop," bring us back to the theme of productivity. These proverbs are consistent with the large number of American idioms that emphasize perpetual activity. Examples include: "How are you doing?" along with the routine responses, "Keeping busy," "Doing fine." Benjamin Franklin's succinct comment, "Speak little, do much," sums this value up.

As you can see from this exercise, there definitely is such a thing as American culture. Certainly it is a way of life woven from the threads of diverse peoples, but it is, nonetheless, a true culture with its own values, style, and ways of looking at the world. (More information on American culture will be found in subsequent chapters, as well as in the appendixes and Supplementary Reading list.)

These two exercises, as well as others found in the discussion of cross-cultural training techniques (chapter 6), serve two important functions. First, they help us become aware of our own cultures, and, in turn, improve our ability to perceive accurately the immigrant and ethnic worker. Second, the increased self-awareness these exercises encourage provides an enriching opportunity to know ourselves better, make more informed choices, and appreciate the strengths and virtues of our own unique cultures.

Don't Overdo: Adapt Rather Than Adopt

As important as it is to become conscious of your culture and aware of your own cultural point of view, this does not mean

Final

that you are expected to change that culture radically or discard it. It is all right to like and value your own ways, and, in fact, studies have shown that appreciating one's own values and way of life does not make a person any more likely to be critical of other cultures.

Managers need to be reassured that although they are being called upon to make adjustments and compromises in their interactions with culturally different workers, they are not being asked to change their essential personalities and cultural perspectives. The point of this book is that there are adaptations to be made. The danger lies, however, in going too far too fast, in giving up cherished values or in adopting behaviors that are insincere and excessively uncomfortable. Some of the consequences of this "cultural overkill" are these:

1. *Immigrant and ethnic workers might feel patronized*. Culturally different workers appreciate respect, understanding, and compromise. They do not, however, expect the manager to adopt the specific features of their culture or, to use the nineteenth-century phrase, "go native." For the manager to, say, look away just because the Asian is more comfortable with indirect eye contact or stand very close to the Middle Eastern male because that is the way it is done in the Middle East can be perceived of as patronizing and insincere.

2. *Misunderstandings might result*. In efforts to assimilate into our culture, immigrant and ethnic workers are learning about American values and behaviors just as we are learning about theirs. Filipino workers, for example, know that in America it is expected, within certain limits, that workers speak up about their achievements and skills. They also know that when Americans are self-effacing, it often means that they are lacking in confidence and self-esteem.

Filipinos have been taught to behave very differently. For them, it is more appropriate to be modest and let their work speak for itself. If managers try to please Filipinos by adopting this approach, appearing artificially self-effacing and modest, they are in danger of getting an unexpected reaction. The Filipino worker, wisely, is going to interpret the manager's behavior in the context of American culture; after all the manager is a product of that culture. The result would be that the worker would quickly conclude that the manager is indeed lacking in confidence and possibly even ability.

3. *Managers are likely to feel resentment.* Just as the immigrant and ethnic worker has a right to his or her values, so does the native-born or assimilated manager. When people pretend to be something they are not, it often creates resentment, which is eventually manifested in the form of negative feelings toward those whom they are trying to imitate. If, for example, managers began eating Vietnamese food in the cafeteria not because they chose to but because they felt pressured into doing so, a backlash would develop that could interfere with good working relationships.

4. *Resentment on the part of other workers will develop.* Giving preferential treatment to any one group can cause resentment among other groups. It is one thing to be culturally sensitive and respectful but quite another to go overboard on behalf of one culture. In chapter 2, for example, it is suggested that managers learn a few words of their workers' languages. If this is done, it should be done for every group in the workplace so as to avoid the accusation of preferential treatment.

5. *The opportunity to teach the ways of American culture will be missed.* One of the best ways to teach the nuances of a culture is to model that culture—to live it in front of those whom you wish to teach. No amount of verbiage will pass on the true style of a culture along with its subtle rules and expectations as well as watching that style being acted out. By pretending to be something you are not and abandoning your culture, you lose a valuable chance to help others understand that culture better.

6. *Embarrassing mistakes can be made.* In many ways, learning about cultures is easy. There are rules and insights that can be readily applied and that make a real difference in how effectively we get along with others. On a deeper level, however, culture is subtle and replete with nuances of behavior that are difficult to grasp intellectually and almost impossible to perform. Be yourself. By trying to be something you are not, you are risking errors in etiquette and behavior that can be embarrassing

to all concerned. It is far more important that we put our energy into learning to understand other cultures, into making reasonable compromises, and into communicating respect for others and for ourselves.

Summary

These first steps toward bridging cultural barriers are perhaps the most difficult ones to execute. By following the suggestions put forth in this chapter, you will develop a framework of cultural awareness within which the balance of the material can readily be understood.

- Remember that both managers and workers are vulnerable to culture shock.
- Acknowledge differences as well as commonalities.
- Become aware of and set aside stereotypes.
- Remember that stereotypes can be about both positive and negative characteristics.
- Get to know your own culture as well as the cultures of others.
- Do not project your culture onto others.
- Be yourself while communicating respect.
- Be reassured that we are all experienced in cultural diversity; every interaction involves some form of cross-cultural communication.

Notes

1. Paraphrased from R.M. Smith, *Emigration and Immigration* (New York: Charles Scribner's Sons, 1890).
2. R. Benedict, *Patterns of Culture* (Boston: Houghton Mifflin, 1934).
3. R. Benedict, *The Chrysanthemum and the Sword: Patterns of Japanese Culture* (Boston: Houghton Mifflin, 1946).

2
Language Diversity
Achieving Successful Communication

The problem with communication is the illusion that it has been accomplished.

—George Bernard Shaw

This chapter covers:

- The impact of accent and language differences
- Ways of assessing the English-language ability of job applicants
- Techniques for making yourself understood
- Methods for assessing how well you have been understood
- Techniques for understanding the nonnative English speaker
- Ideas for encouraging the speaking of English

More than 110 languages and dialects are spoken in the United States today, and 11 percent of the population speaks a language other than English in the home. This remarkable diversity is creating considerable confusion for both immigrants and English-speaking Americans. Managers are concerned that workers do not comprehend safety instructions, trainers are having difficulty determining if their material is being understood, human-resource professionals are often confused about how to assess the foreign-language-speaking applicant, and personnel managers are muddled about what it means when applicants bring family members to assist with the completion of forms.

Much can be done to communicate effectively with workers who possess heavy accents or even with those who speak an unfamiliar language. The purpose of this chapter is to help human-resource professionals and, in turn, managers, to do just that: to achieve successful two-way communication with foreign-born workers and colleagues.

Understanding the Immigrant's Perspective

One important step in this direction is for managers to put themselves in the immigrant's position and attempt to under-stand what it feels like to be in a new country and not speak the language. Also many workers in American industry who were born in the United States have yet to learn the language. The material in this chapter is applicable to those employees as well.

Do exercise 2–1 and then offer it to managers within the organization. It requires taking a moment to recall a time when you, like immigrant workers, were immersed in a foreign setting, surrounded by a strange culture, and confronted with an unfa-miliar language. Although situations like these might generate some excitement, they also produce several uncomfortable emo-tions. Listed in the exercise are some of these feelings. Circle the numbers to indicate which of these emotions you have experi-enced when in another culture and to what degree. Mark the lowest numbers if you felt little or none of the feeling and higher numbers if the feeling was intense.

Exercise 2–1
Emotions Experienced in a Strange Culture

Loneliness	1	2	3	4	5	6	7	8	9	10
Fear	1	2	3	4	5	6	7	8	9	10
Passivity	1	2	3	4	5	6	7	8	9	10
Inadequacy	1	2	3	4	5	6	7	8	9	10

Readers who circled number 6 or higher in two or more of

these categories have a good grasp of what it feels like to be surrounded by a culture and a language that are foreign and confusing. Remember, too, that the travels you have just recalled were probably temporary sojourns overseas. Imagine how magnified these feelings would have become if you were attempting to build a permanent home in a new land.

These emotions are not just unpleasant; they can interfere with one's functioning in society. Loneliness, for example, and the desire for companionship are among the primary reasons for the speaking of foreign languages in the workplace.

Fear also has an effect on behavior. We are talking here about the kind of fear we have all felt when confronted with a strange environment: perhaps fear of not getting our needs met, fear of being misunderstood, fear of making mistakes, or even fear of being laughed at because of the way we express ourselves. Educators and trainers are aware that this sort of anxiety, which many immigrants experience, can interfere with the ability to concentrate and learn in the training room.

Fear can also give rise to passivity. How often have you found yourself in a foreign country wanting to go to a new restaurant but too shy to risk the embarrassment of not being able to interpret the menu? For immigrants, this type of incapacitation can have far more serious consequences than a missed meal. A foreign-language-speaking worker may fail to take independent initiative on a task partially because he or she is afraid of having misunderstood the supervisor's instructions. As we shall see in the chapters to come, this sort of passivity can easily be misinterpreted as weakness, cowardice, or even laziness.

Have you ever felt inadequate when you could not speak the language of those around you? When people who are educated, intelligent, and reasonably accomplished and who rely on their ability to demonstrate those virtues verbally are unable to make themselves understood, they appear to others to be slow, unimaginative, and undeducated. Thousands of foreign-born professionals who are entering the United States today are experiencing this same difficulty. They may appear to be inarticulate and inexperienced—perceptions that often generate feelings of inadequacy and low self-esteem.

Lack of English-language facility can also interfere with workers' ability to understand instructions, to grasp the values of American culture, and to receive the promotions and praise for which they are otherwise qualified. The results are lowered confidence and, consequently, lowered feelings of self-worth.

Clearly the consequences of having undeveloped English-language facility extend far beyond simply not being able to speak with others. Let us look at some of the misconceptions surrounding this problem and then move on to some specific ways in which communication can be improved.

Undeveloped English-Language Facility: Getting the Facts Straight

What happens when managers hear workers or colleagues speak with foreign accents? Do they immediately assume that the speaker is uneducated and incapable of understanding what is being said? Do they find themselves judging the accent and not listening to the speaker's words? What about those times when an immigrant declares that he or she understands what is being said, only to have it turn out that this was not the case? Does the manager feel lied to and betrayed?

These and other misconceptions about what language and accent differences mean can interfere with efforts to communicate effectively. Following are the most common misunderstandings that occur in the face of language diversity:

Misconception: Listeners mistakenly believe that workers with heavy foreign accents are likely to be uneducated, unassimilated into American culture, of low socioeconomic status, and ignorant of English vocabulary and grammar.

The True Picture: An accent tells us very little about the speaker.

Although there are times when these assumptions are accurate, more often than not they amount to nothing more than rash and incorrect judgments. When we hear a foreign accent, all that we can be certain of is that the speaker is at least bilingual—and in today's shrinking world, that is likely to be a definite asset.

Those of us who have attempted to learn foreign languages know, much to our dismay, that it is far easier to learn the vocabulary and grammar of a language than it is to master correct pronunciation. This is particularly true of immigrants whose native tongues do not share the Germanic and Romantic roots of English. Asians and Southeast Asians, for example, have greater difficulty pronouncing English than do Hispanics, whose native Spanish developed, like English, out of the Romance languages. This difficulty lies primarily in the fact that English uses sounds other languages lack. The Japanese, for example, have no sounds that correspond to our *l* or *r*. What they do have is one sound that falls somewhere in between the two. For this reason, many Japanese cannot hear an English *l* and *r*, much less pronounce them. Similarly, Arabic speakers have difficulty with the English *g* and *j*; Filipinos with *b*, *v*, *p*, and *ph*; and Farsi (Iranian)-speaking immigrants *v* and *w*.

This pronunciation problem is made worse by the nonphonetic spelling of many English words. As a result, the correct pronunciation of words such as *character*, *school*, and *handkerchief* can be a problem for even the most educated immigrants.

English is difficult to pronounce, and many competent professionals never completely overcome the challenges. Clearly when we come across a worker who speaks with an accent, we need to resist the temptation to make any snap judgments about that person's background or abilities.

Misconception: If an immigrant cannot speak much English, he or she probably is unable to understand much either.

The True Picture: It is far easier for immigrants to understand English than to speak the language themselves.

We have seen that English is difficult to pronounce and that it is far easier to learn correct vocabulary and grammar than it is to master many English sounds. Similarly, a person attempting to acquire a new language finds that the first thing that comes together is the ability to comprehend what is said. It takes some time for the skill of speaking the language to catch up with the ability to understand. In short, the fact that an immigrant may not speak much English does not mean that he or she does not understand what is being said.

> *Misconception*: Once vocabulary and grammar are learned, the immigrant will always understand what is being said.

> *The True Picture*: There is more to understanding a language than just knowing vocabulary and grammar.

It is a fairly simple matter to know the literal translation of English words but much more difficult to grasp the subtleties and shades of meaning in these words. English is riddled with subtleties, many of them difficult to grasp unless one is raised in this culture. The following pairs of sentences, each representing two entirely different meanings, will give a good idea of the complexity of English:

1. Dick did not come to work today.
   Dick did not show up for work today.

2. The speaker elaborated the point for an hour.
   The speaker belabored the point for an hour.

3. Abraham Lincoln was a wise man.
   Abraham Lincoln was a wise guy.

Although all the vocabulary in these sentences might be understood by the nonnative speaker, the dramatic differences in meaning could easily be lost.

Another nuance of the language involves English phrases that, if taken literally, can create additional confusion for the foreign born. "You can say that again" and "It's just one of those things," for example, are merely cultural commonplaces that are not meant to be acted on or explored further. Cole

Porter, the composer who popularized the latter phrase, never intended for the listener to respond by asking, "What things?" nor would it be appropriate to go ahead and "say it again." Similarly, "I have a lot of running around to do," could lead the nonnative speaker to think of you as a dedicated athlete. English is littered with such expressions, many of which can create painful embarrassment if taken literally.

Worse, sometimes the same words have an opposite meaning depending on the context. To say, "I believe in this idea" connotes a firm commitment to the concept. On the other hand, to respond "I believe so" to a question connotes some doubt about the matter. The questions "Would you like something to drink?" and "Would you like a drink?" carry with them quite different meanings. The first query offers any kind of beverage, whereas the second implies the availability of alcohol.

Such social convention reaches an extreme in the query, "Why don't you read this over?" This statement, if taken at face value, might be interpreted either as a question to be answered or as an attack: "What is the matter with you? Why don't you get on with it and read this over?" In fact, etiquette tells us that this is merely a gentle way of inviting the listener to read the material; it might be rephrased, "Please read this over." As you can see, there is a great deal more to understanding what is intended than just knowing the vocabulary.

Misconception: Foreigners are often rude, harsh, and demanding.

The True Picture: Sometimes the intonation of the speaker's native language along with the lack of softening phrases can make the immigrant sound inadvertently rude.

Although the speaker may feel no hostility and does not intend to sound demanding or abrupt, the intonation of his or her original language may not convert well to English. When the speaker of a northern Indian dialect attempts English, the tone tends to sound harsh and abrupt to American ears. A Middle Easterner may sound a bit loud and brusk, whereas the softer tone of many Asians may leave an equally inaccurate impression of meekness or fear. These examples illustrate the importance of understanding cultural differences in the style or tone of speech.

These misunderstandings may be amplified when the speaker is unfamiliar with how to use the softening words and phrases of English, devices important to smoothing the social process. Many languages do not have the equivalent of words like *could*, *might*, or *may*, each crucial in cushioning the impact of a demand. Note the difference in tone between the following pairs of sentences:

1. Fill the order right now.
   I'd appreciate your filling the order as soon as possible.

2. Get me the invoices from the drawer.
   Could you get the invoices from the drawer?

3. This work is no good.
   There are some problems with this work.

The tone of these sentences changes through the careful choice of words and phrases. In some languages, this softening effect is achieved not through the addition of words but through the adjustment of verbs, word order, and pronoun forms. French and German rely heavily on the choice of pronouns to achieve subtleties of meaning. Japanese uses varying verb forms to obtain the same results. In the Philippines the prefix *paki-* is added to verbs to distinguish a request from a command.

Learning proper intonation is possibly the most difficult part of mastering a new language. If you add to this the necessity of understanding how and when to use softening words and phrases, it is no wonder that the emotions and intent of many foreign-born workers and colleagues are often misunderstood.

Misconception: When immigrants speak their native language around those who do not understand it, they do so out of laziness and/or out of a desire to exclude outsiders.

The True Picture: Immigrants speak their native language

usually as a means of relieving feelings of isolation and/or in response to a crisis.

Managers of foreign-born workers sometimes become concerned when they discover that foreign languages are spoken in the workplace. Depending on the setting, this behavior can cause fellow workers to feel excluded, customers and clients to lose confidence, and managers to feel incapable of communicating effectively.

As disruptive as this behavior can be, it usually does not arise out of a desire to be hostile or exclusive. Most likely, the speaking of a foreign language serves one or more of the following functions:

1. It helps to relieve feelings of isolation and loneliness.
2. It allows the worker to relax for a few moments. Constantly speaking a new language can be a great strain.
3. It allows the worker to function efficiently in a crisis.

This is not to say that speaking a foreign language in the workplace does not sometimes create difficulties but merely that it is usually not the hostile act it is often assumed to be. Also, it is important that you keep in mind any legal restrictions against insisting that only English be spoken in the workplace.

Misconception: When immigrants pretend to understand what has been said, they are doing so as an act of deceit.

The True Picture: Pretending to understand usually reflects a desire to avoid embarrassment for all concerned.

The problem with this behavior is that it leaves the speaker with no way of knowing whether a message has gotten across. Because of the importance of this topic, an entire section of this chapter has been devoted to techniques for assessing how much understanding has actually taken place. In addition, this problem will be touched upon in various connections throughout the book.

Assessing English-Language Abilities

Depending on the duties of the position, personnel interviewers must sometimes assess how much English foreign-born and ethnic applicants understand, speak, read, and write. Someone who has not had to make a fairly quick judgment about a person's English-language facility may think this a simple task. But those who have hired employees, only to discover that they have great difficulty speaking to customers or understanding instructions, realize that this is not as easy as it looks. The following tips will be helpful:

1. Ask the worker to complete the job application in your office and to do so alone. This negates the possibility of the applicant's getting help from a family member or friend and therefore allows you to assess more accurately how well he or she read the instructions and filled out the form.

2. Have some of the instructions on the application be a bit more complex than just "name," "address," and "education." The applicant may be familiar with those words from previous experience; lengthier instructions serve as a better test of the ability to read English.

3. Include a request for a short essay somewhere on the application so that the worker will be forced to demonstrate English writing skills.

4. Engage the applicant in extensive conversation in order to tell how much English is spoken and understood. The techniques found at the end of this chapter are useful for encouraging this exchange.

Making Yourself Understood

Now that you have a good grasp of what language diversity is all about, let us move on to some ways in which to minimize the impact of these differences. Each of the following situations illustrates techniques that will help you communicate more successfully to workers whose English is not fully developed. As you and your managers attempt to pick the answer that seems best, remember that some of the situations have more than one right solution and some of the answers are subject to debate. After you have chosen your answer or answers, find out how well you have done by looking below each example at the discussion of the various options. Good luck; be creative, and trust your instincts.

Situation 1—The Simple Solutions: Barbara is a manager at a large hotel and resort complex. In this capacity, she works with Southeast Asian employees who sometimes have difficulty understanding what she is saying. On one occasion, a middle-aged Vietnamese woman seemed especially confused. To relieve the situation, Barbara should have:

a. Spoken more loudly because the woman was probably hard of hearing

b. Spoken more slowly and distinctly

c. Spoken pidgin English and emphasized the key words so that it would be easier for the woman to understand

d. Allowed longer pauses in the conversation

e. Tried to keep the woman from reading her lips because to do so just creates confusion

Evaluating the Options

a. Although the woman might have been hard of hearing, it is safer to assume, at least initially, that this is not the case. There is, of course, a natural tendency to raise one's voice when not being understood. The problem with doing so prematurely is that it can frighten an immigrant who is already intimidated by not understanding what is being said.

This is particularly a problem when dealing with Asians,

who regard a raised voice as disruptive of social harmony. In situations like this, the Asian is likely to speak softer as the American speaks louder. The cycle continues, much to the frustration and discomfort of both parties.

b. *This is a good answer.* Americans generally talk fast, a trait considered a sign of brightness and enthusiasm in the business world. Not only do we speak too rapidly for many immigrants to understand, but we also tend to run words together and pronounce them incompletely. To ask, for example, "Whatdjasay?" is all very well, but it will not elicit much information from someone who does not have a great deal of proficiency in English. Similarly "Didjaeetyet?" will be meaningless to even the hungriest nonnative speaker. Try to be aware of your speech and to enunciate carefully even the most commonplace words.

Note: While we are on the subject of enunciation, it is best to minimize the use of "uh huh" and "uh uh" for "yes" and "no." For one thing, these sounds can be indistinct and difficult to decipher; in addition, the Tagalog word for "yes" sounds dangerously close to the English slang term "uh uh" for "no."

c. This option is not fair to readers because if you chose it, you are half-right and half-wrong. On the one hand, pidgin English should be avoided. Sentences like "You fill out application, you get job" are not easier to understand and are insulting to intelligent applicants. On the other hand, emphasizing key words can be helpful to the worker who understands English but tends to get lost in the verbiage. Be careful not to raise your voice too much when emphasizing these words and ideas; that will intimidate the worker and discourage good communication.

d. *This is an excellent answer.* Just as American culture encourages rapid speech, it discourages pauses in the conversation. We think of silence as threatening and a sign of failure or lack of communication. But many other cultures regard silence as a demonstration of strength, as a way of communicating respect for what the speaker has just said, and as an opportunity to formulate well-thought-out comments and questions. The Japanese proverb, "He who speaks does not know; he who knows does not speak" exemplifies the perspective found in many Far

Eastern countries. The practical ramification is that the non-English speaker needs time in which to digest what has been said and in which to formulate a response.

If you find it difficult to maintain silence, use those few moments to take some deep breaths, compose a particularly intelligent comment of your own, or simply to enjoy a period of quiet. It might help to remember that Thomas Carlyle said, "Silence is more eloquent than words."

e. This is not such a good answer. There is nothing confusing about allowing the listener to see your lips as you speak. In fact, this is a good way to help the nonnative speaker decipher what you are saying.

Situation 2—Training: Tom trains dozens of foreign-born and ethnic workers at the corporate office of a large midwestern bank. He has a great deal of enthusiasm for both the material and the training process. Although he is fairly unorganized, Tom brings lots of energy to the training class by interjecting interesting anecdotes and digressions. He also uses slides and handouts extensively. His supervisor has begun to complain that some of the trainees do not seem to be retaining much of the material. What could be the problem?

   a. The problem probably lies with the slides. Too much sensory input can confuse foreign-born trainees.
   b. Tom should be more organized. His digressions, although interesting, can obscure the main points he is trying to make.
   c. Perhaps the difficulty lies with the handouts. Too many teaching aids can overwhelm students who do not speak English very well.

Evaluating the Options

   a. Probably this is not the problem. Visual aids that are legible, simple, and clear will help all students. Each of us learns with the aid of our senses. The more senses that are utilized—in this case, hearing and sight—the more rapidly will learning take place.

b. *This is the best answer.* Although spontaneity and enthusiasm are virtues in an instructor, excessive asides can be confusing to trainees struggling to understand what is being said. Also, the fact that Tom is fairly unorganized probably means that he is not allowing enough time at the end of the class in which to recap the covered material. The process of review is extremely important in any training setting; it is vital when dealing with immigrant workers.

c. Probably this is not the problem. As we shall see shortly, the written word is an important tool in cross-cultural communication. Any material the trainee misses in class can be picked up by reading the handouts.

> **Situation 3—The Telephone:** Doing business on the telephone is Richard's strength; he has an outgoing personality and is a good communicator. Richard puts these talents to use daily as the manager in charge of dozens of workers scattered throughout his plant. He spends a great deal of time on the telephone, giving instructions and keeping tabs on things.
>
> Sometimes, though, Richard is not sure that he is being understood. Many of his best workers are in the process of learning English, and he sometimes does not know if his message has gotten across. The problem came to a head when Richard thought he had given clear instructions for an important project, only to discover on follow-up that the task had been done incorrectly. What might Richard have done to prevent this costly misunderstanding?
>
> > a. There is not much he could have done. Since roughly 50 percent of all communication is visual—that is, through body language—telephone conversations, even in the absence of language differences, are fraught with the risk of misunderstanding.
> >
> > b. The errors had nothing to do with language facil-

ity. This was the sort of mix-up that could have happened between any manager and worker.

c. Since this was such an important project and because Richard knew there was the danger of misunderstanding, he should have followed up each telephone call with a written memo repeating his instructions.

Evaluating the Options

a. Although conversation is more difficult on the telephone, there is still much that can be done to ensure accurate communication. Try another answer.

b. In some ways, this is a good choice. It is important that we not get so preoccupied with cross-cultural issues that we forget about the ordinary principles of effective communication—principles that can be applied in any setting.

c. *This is an excellent answer.* It is easier to understand the written than the spoken word. In all areas of business, the use of written memos after important telephone calls and conversations can alleviate many misunderstandings and disappointments. The same applies to meetings and interviews. A detailed agenda and follow-up document can go far toward minimizing the embarrassment and dismay that lack of understanding can cause. Posting important memos regarding benefits, policy changes, or company events on the bulletin board can also help minimize cross-cultural communication problems.

Situation 4—Gestures: Susan loves her work as a manager at a large electronics firm. The aspect she likes most about her position is that she has the opportunity to meet and work with many different types of people. In recent years, her work force has become particularly diverse with growing numbers of immigrant and ethnic employees.

Although she enjoys the diversity, Susan sometimes finds herself gesturing a great deal in order to communicate. During one recent performance appraisal, she indicated to a South American worker that he was doing well by giving him the "OK" gesture. The worker seemed embarrassed and offended. He was probably upset because:

a. Susan had inadvertently made a hand gesture that carries sexual connotations in South America.

b. Susan used her hands and facial expressions to communicate. In South America it is considered inappropriate for women to gesture and be expressive.

c. Susan is a woman, and South Americans generally do not allow women into management positions.

Evaluating the Options

a. *This is the best answer*. Although body language is an adjunct to successful cross-cultural communication, we must be careful not to use gestures that can offend people from other cultures. As Susan discovered, the "OK" sign is one of these potentially offensive signals.

Body language, along with tone of voice, is powerful. It can improve relations with nonnative workers—and it can offend these employees. This is particularly true when someone is disoriented by a culture and/or does not know the language. Disorientation causes the individual to be very attuned to all nonverbal signals. In addition, some cultures, such as many Asian and Middle Eastern groups, place greater store on what they see and on the way words are spoken than on the words themselves. To them it is not so much what is said that is important, but how it is said. This is in contrast to American culture, where words are often the only thing considered.

b. This is an incorrect answer. Using the hands and face to communicate is largely accepted among Latin cultures. Asian cultures, however, are different. In many Far Eastern countries, women are expected to keep facial expressions and hand gestures to a minimum. To do otherwise is to appear undignified and to call excessive attention to the individual.

c. Probably this was not the difficulty. It is true that there are still gender barriers, but immigrant communities generally accept American women as legitimate business professionals who are worthy of both attention and respect.

Situation 5—Choosing Your Words: Jane manages a work force that is approximately 60 percent Hispanic. Most of the workers have been in the United States for some time so have come to speak English fairly well. They still, however, have some difficulty understanding Jane's instructions.

Jane does not speak Spanish but has devised some techniques for communicating better. She tries to use English words that are similar to their Spanish equivalent; she tries to notice the English terms her workers use and understand and use those same words when giving instructions; and she is very careful, when demonstrating a procedure, to say what she is going to do, do it, and then repeat the instructions. What do you think of Jane's approach?

a. It seems to me that using English words with Spanish equivalents and words that the speaker already understands will only slow down the process of learning English.

b. I do not think there is any problem with Jane's using English words with Spanish equivalents, and it also seems as if this is a good way to boost the workers' confidence in their ability to understand English.

c. Repeating instructions before and after a procedure seems patronizing. It is as if Jane assumes that they won't understand.

Evaluating the Options

a. This is not a good answer. Any technique that allows nonnative speakers to communicate successfully in English is a good one. The more they understand, the more confidence they will have and the more willing they will be to continue to speak English.

Note: Some examples of Spanish words that are similar in English are *banco*, *client*, *doctor*, *hospital*, *hotel*, *distancia*, *diferente*, *complicado*, and *cancelar*. The English equivalents are just what they appear to be.

b. *This is an excellent answer*. Success breeds success. Not only will using techniques such as these encourage the speaking of English, but it will also lead to the successful completion of tasks and the building of confidence in all areas.

c. It is hard to be certain if this answer is correct. There is not enough information supplied in the scenario to tell us what Jane is feeling. If Jane is excessively pessimistic about her workers' abilities to understand, it will show, and her repetition of the instructions will probably be perceived of as patronizing. But if she has a genuine desire to help and to build a productive team, this feeling will be clear to the employees, and her careful approach will be seen as respectful and compassionate.

> **Situation 6—Making Meetings Work:** Kitty is a senior manager at a large firm in the Southwest. Because of the location of the company, most of Kitty's management staff were born and raised in Mexico. The majority of these managers, however, have a fair working knowledge of English.
>
> Kitty likes to hold management meetings regularly but has difficulty getting everyone together at the same time. For this reason, she holds intermittent gatherings, which are very long and deal with many issues at a sitting. At the end of each meeting, Kitty checks with the managers to make certain they have understood what has taken place. Often she discovers that they do not. What could be the problem, and how might it be solved?
>
> a. Rather than waiting until the end of the meeting to ask if the material is being understood, Kitty should do so at various points along the way.
>
> b. There would be more comprehension if the meetings were shorter. Even if Kitty could not cover every topic in a short time, she would probably

come out with a much higher percentage of comprehension.

c. Kitty should have put together a detailed agenda
and follow-up document. This way she could have
taken advantage of the written word to clarify the
most important points.

Evaluating the Options

a. *This is an excellent answer.* When there is any question of
the group's comprehension, it is important to stop frequently to
check for understanding. If a crucial point is missed along the
way, any subsequent information that builds on that point will
be lost as well.

b. *This is also a good answer.* Those who do not speak
English well are struggling to perform two tasks at once: they
are trying to understand the words being said and to remember
the important concepts. For this reason, fatigue is likely to set in
fairly rapidly. Shorter sessions will prove more comfortable and
more productive.

c. *You cannot lose on this one.* As we have discovered, the
written word is valuable in many cross-cultural situations. The
agenda would have alerted the managers as to what to listen for,
and the follow-up document would have provided a second opportunity for understanding.

Situation 7—Using the System: Roberta supervises a
work force that is approximately 15 percent Cambodian,
10 percent Laotion, 5 percent Korean, 30 percent Cuban,
10 percent Iranian, 15 percent Chinese, and the rest
native-born Americans. Her workers range widely in their
ability to understand English, although each group has a
few informal leaders who are bilingual. Roberta's problem is that many of the workers are not taking advantage
of the company's benefits partly because they do not
understand them. What might Roberta do to solve this
difficulty?

a. She should translate the benefits into the languages
of her workers.

    b. She should explain the benefits to the bilingual group leaders and have them spread the information among their countrymen.

    c. She should call in interpreters and use them to explain the benefits to the workers.

Evaluating the Options

a. This is a satisfactory answer, although it is not always the panacea that it appears to be. Translation is a difficult task; dialects vary, idioms are confusing, and some words lack equivalents in other languages. There is also the logistical problem of having the information translated into the numerous languages Roberta has in her workplace. Remember that it will appear discriminatory to provide this service for only some of the groups.

Note: When having any material translated, be certain to use someone who is a native speaker of the foreign language but who also knows English very well. He or she should be familiar with both cultures and should be certain to use the correct dialect and idiom. Also, it is important that the level of vocabulary be appropriate to the reader. To assure an accurate translation, have one person convert the words into the desired language, and have someone else translate them back into English. This is a good way to check that you are saying what you really want to say. Stories abound resulting from translation problems, including the classic case of Pepsi Cola's effort to market its product in Europe with the slogan, "Come alive with Pepsi," only to find that it had been translated to read "Come out of the grave with Pepsi."

b. *This is a good answer.* Informal group leaders are a valuable resource for managers and human-resource professionals. They are likely to be bilingual and therefore able to communicate well, and they hold the respect of the group so they can function as valuable conduits between manager and worker.

c. Although not wrong, this answer has some of the problems of *a.* Using interpreters can be cumbersome, they may be hard to find, and, worse, they may not be very good. There is a great deal more to being a good interpreter than simply knowing two languages. It is also necessary to know the cultures and personalities involved so that the nuances of the information can be properly communicated.

Each of these case studies has illustrated simple techniques that will allow managers to communicate better with immigrant and foreign language-speaking workers and colleagues. To review briefly:

- Do not shout.
- Speak slowly and distinctly.
- Avoid pidgin English.
- Emphasize key words.
- Allow pauses.
- Let the worker read your lips.
- Use visual aids.
- Organize your thoughts.
- Use the written word and handouts.
- Use nonverbal signals (cautiously).
- Be aware of your tone of voice.
- Use familiar words.
- Repeat and recap frequently.
- Take care not to patronize.
- Check for understanding frequently.
- Do not cover too much information at one time.
- Be careful when translating.
- Choose interpreters carefully.
- Use bilingual group leaders.

The most important tip of all, however, was only briefly alluded to: choose your words and construct your sentences carefully so that they communicate precisely what you want as clearly as possible. Because this task is not as easy as it sounds, a separate section as been devoted to the topic of how to make your English more precise and more intelligible.

Your English: Some Tips for Greater Clarity

The tips provided here are applicable to any interaction, not just to those involving workers whose native language is not English.

It would be lovely if everyone would minimize jargon, be more concrete and organized in speaking, use shorter words, and keep their sentences uncomplicated.

Idioms, Slang, and Jargon

Idioms and slang have long been a part of the English language. In the nineteenth century, "How goes the enemy?" was a common way of asking for the time. Around 1900, to inquire, "How's your belly for spots?" usually received a polite "I'm fine, thank you." In the second half of this century, Americans have been variously concerned with "What's cooking?" "What's up doc?" and "What's shaking?" Some have even been known to ask "What's your poison?" when offering a drink and "What's the damage?" when requesting the cost of a product or service.

Jargon, too, has been with us for centuries. Words we take for granted today were once industry terms designed to meet the needs of a new technology. *Typewriter, airplane,* and *automobile* are the most obvious examples. Today's jargon includes *turbo charged, lift-off, bytes, telemarketing,* and *multicultural.*

If we add to this the proliferation of acronyms in our vocabulary, it is not surprising that even native-English speakers at times have little idea of what is being said. For immigrants, the situation is worse. We tend to forget that jargon, slang, and idioms are rarely taught in English-as-a-second-language classes.

The danger with informal English is that we use such terms too often and far too unconsciously. The speech in Exercise 2–2 contains examples of idioms, slang, and jargon. Take a moment to circle each one. "Take your time," "Go for it," "Have a ball," and "Hang in there."

Exercise 2–2. Identifying Idioms, Slang, and Jargon

[*Will, a middle-level manager, is addressing a group of new employees, many of whom do not speak English very well. Will's purpose is to welcome the workers to the company and orient them to the plant.*]

Thanks a million for showing up on time and a heart-felt "thank you" to every last one of the staff who took the time to set up the room so nicely. Of course, it would stand to reason that I could count on a team like ours. I have gotten feedback that a lot of elbow grease was called for in getting this show on the road.

It's been on my mind for some time now to say a word or two about the company's corporate culture and give you a feel for the tasks you will be facing in the weeks ahead. I don't want to bring you down, but I have to lay it on the line by spelling it out that we are behind schedule and that we are, on the whole, going to have to move into high gear and work around the clock to catch up.

As you can see, I am not one to make light of or gloss over what clearly is a full-fledged crisis. It is beyond question but that we should not throw in the towel. One thing you can bank on: there will be no layoffs, and, although the next few weeks will see us all with our noses to the grindstone, take heart from knowing that management will make an all-out effort to back you up and see to it that you carry on and make it to the finish line.

Let me put your minds at rest—although we have our hands full, we will make do, keep our heads, and get back on our feet. By taking charge of the task and by getting a head start on the competition, we cannot help but come out ahead.

How did you do? Maybe it will help if you know that there are fifty examples of slang and idioms in the passage. Some of these examples are obvious and some more subtle. When you have circled your selection, look over the following list; you may be surprised at what you find.

thanks a million	high gear
showing up	around the clock
on time	catch up
heart-felt	make light of
every last one	gloss over

took the time	full-fledged
set up	beyond question
of course	throw in the towel
stand to reason	bank on
count on	layoffs
feedback	noses to the grindstone
elbow grease	take heart
called for	an all out show
on the road	back you up on
my mind	see to it
a word or two	carry on
corporate culture	finish line
a feel for	minds at rest
be facing	hands full
bring you down	make do
have to	keep our heads
lay it on the line	get back on your feet
spelling out	taking charge
behind schedule	head start on
the whole	come out

Some of these phrases are easy to spot. We are probably fairly conscious of choosing idioms like "elbow grease" and "thanks a million." Most idioms, however, are such an integral part of everyday speech that they are used unconsciously. Actually there is no problem with this as long as the usage is understood by the listener. Try to remember, however, that even the most worldly foreign-language speaker is likely to become muddled when told to "bide your time," "play it cool," or "give it your best shot." Sadly, many cases have been reported in which workers were "fired" or "let go," only to return to the job the next day because they did not understand the jargon.

In addition to being alert to your choice of words, it is also helpful to construct an easy-to-understand glossary of industry jargon, which can be distributed to all new employees. We all find it embarrassing to have to ask the meaning of a term, particularly if we feel that it is a word we ought to know. It would be most unpleasant, for example, for a hospital worker to become confused over the meaning of LOC, a term that, in different parts of the country, variously means "level of consciousness" or "laxative of choice." A glossary would eliminate—or at least minimize—the need to ask. Your effort, and that of your managers, would be appreciated by workers who are uncomfortable with the loss of face that accompanies having to ask the meaning of terms ranging from "flextime" to "deductible," "exempt," or, sadly, "laid-off."

Keeping It Simple

Most of us have lost track of what simple, straightforward expression is all about. Big words, complex sentences, and, worst of all, too much verbiage have become the rule in our culture. Speaking and writing in complex sentences is a habit we usually indulge in unconsciously. Fortunately, practice, such as that provided in exercise 2–3, can help a great deal. It will make you and your managers aware of the bad habits that compromise the ability to communicate with immigrant workers. Read over the passages and try to recompose each one in a more easily understood style. When you are finished, examine the options provided and see how well you did.

Exercise 2–3 Simplifying Your English

1. "If you study this manual, follow the instructions provided by your supervisor, stick to the dress code, and are careful about punctuality, you will probably be considered for a promotion."

Your rephrasing:

2. "I was wondering how you found your last position. I once had a friend who worked at that company, until one day

they told her that they felt she would be happier working else-where."

Your rephrasing:

3. "We are barely going to make that deadline. I almost think we ought to call in several additional workers."

Your rephrasing:

4. "Your employment application is one of the most quintessential ones that I have ever perused. Your plethora of experiences, your perspicuous abilities, and your extensive academic background clearly make you qualified for this formidable post."

Your rephrasing:

5. "I was told by my boss that it was necessary for me to have you seen by a doctor to make sure you weren't hurt in that fall."

Your rephrasing:

6. "Don't load the red boxes, and be careful not to forget about our early day tomorrow."

Your rephrasing:

7. "What I want you to start doing is to take all the cards out of this box, put them in alphabetical order, and refile them by name in the file against the wall, and be careful not to bend them as they will eventually be sent out to customers, and we certainly want them to look as nice as they do now."

Your rephrasing:

8. "What matters in a situation such as this is that you never again fail to complete the patient's chart at the end of your shift. This effort will be greatly appreciated by myself and by my superiors and will most certainly be reflected in our feeling better about your work than we have in the past. It will also look extremely good on your record and in the eyes of your colleagues, and may eventually result in a promotion or at least a better position."

Your rephrasing:

9. "Locking up is really important when you are working on the night shift. Also, when you first arrive, remember to check that all the machines are clean. When you leave, be sure to put the tools back where they are stored. When you take a break, you must indicate this on your time sheet, and when you first come to work, lock your belongings in your locker."

Your rephrasing:

Simplifying your English is not as easy as it first appears. Let us examine some ways in which these passages might have been rewritten and then discuss the particular problems found within each one:

1. *An Option*: "There are four things you need to do in order to be considered for a promotion: first, study the manual; second, follow instructions; third, abide by the dress code; fourth, be punctual."

   The Issue: Mixing topics in one sentence can be confusing. Stick to one subject at a time or list them systematically.

2. *An Option*: "Did you like your last job? I had a friend who worked at that company until she was asked to leave."

   The Issue: First, these sentences contain confusing idioms. "How did you *find* your last job?" for example, could mean anything from "How did you locate your last job?" to "How did you like your last job?"

   This passage is also extremely vague. Phrases like "she would be happier working elsewhere" do not provide any information and only confuse the listener, who is left thinking about how nice the company was to be so concerned about your friend's happiness. Another example of a vague question is, "How did things go today?" Try to be concrete when you speak, and ask specifically for what you want.

3. *An Option*: "We will make that deadline but only by a few minutes. I am thinking about calling in three or four additional workers."

   The Issue: Modifiers such as *barely, almost, several, scarcely,* and *mostly* are difficult for nonnative English speakers to understand. It is very hard to learn exactly what words like these mean. What does it really mean to "almost think" or "barely make" something? One of the reasons that many foreign-born workers do poorly on multiple-choice examinations is that they tend to include vague modifiers such as these.

4. *An Option*: "Your application is very good. You have a lot of experience, skill, and education. You are certainly qualified for this job."

   The Issue: Managers should keep their choice of vocabulary simple but not patronizing. Winston Churchill, one of the greatest communicators of the twentieth century, said, "Short words are best, and old words, when short, are best of all."

5. *An Option*: "My boss told me that you should see a doctor to make certain you didn't hurt yourself in that fall."

   The Issue: Use the active voice whenever possible. It is easier to understand and results in a simpler sentence structure.

6. *An Option*: "Load the red boxes on Thursday, and remember we have an early day tomorrow."

   The Issue: Do not use negative phrasing; it is more complicated, uses more words, and can lead to misunderstandings. In the sentence above, for example, there is the danger that what will be heard is the phrase "red boxes," and that they will end up being loaded regardless of what else was said. Also, asking someone "not to forget" something is more confusing than simply saying "remember."

7. *An Option*: "This is what I want you to do. First, take these cards out of the box. Put them in alphabetical order by name. After you've done that, refile them in the file that is against the wall. They will eventually be sent out to customers, so be careful not to bend them."

   The Issue: Keep your sentences short and simple. Run-on sentences are very difficult to understand, especially when they are spoken.

8. *An Option*: "Be certain to complete the patient's chart at the end of the day. I will appreciate it very much."

   The Issue: Do not use too many words, and do not talk too much. We see this happening especially when it is necessary to discipline a worker. Our discomfort shows itself in a tendency to keep talking. More words are not clearer and, in fact, are likely to confuse nonnative English speakers. Thomas Jefferson knew this when he said, "The most valuable of all talents is that of never using two words when one will do."

9. *An Option*: "When you arrive at work, first lock your belongings in the locker, and then check that all the machines are clean. When you take a break, be sure to put the time on your time sheet. When you leave, put all the tools back in the storage area and be certain to lock up."

   The Issue: Put sentences in a logical order so they will be more easily understood. Organize your thoughts before you begin, and avoid the temptation of going off into tangents, no matter how interesting they might be.

It may seem like a monumental chore to keep all these rules in mind as you go about the already difficult task of communicating across accent and language barriers. Be assured, however, that speaking more clearly and concisely is very much a matter of habit and practice. If taken one step at a time, the task of good communication, like any other, can be easily accomplished. Here is a quick recap of the contents of this section:

- Avoid idioms, jargon, and slang.
- Talk about one topic at a time.
- Be concrete when you speak.
- Avoid vague modifiers.
- Use simple vocabulary and sentence structure.
- Use the active voice.
- Use positive phrasing.
- Use short sentences.

- Use as few words as possible.
- Keep your topics in a logical order.

Assessing How Well You Have Been Understood

George Bernard Shaw once said, "The greatest problem with communication is the illusion that it has been accomplished." Never before has this been so true as in our multicultural society, where misunderstandings are common and where it is not unusual for workers to pretend to understand when, in fact, they have little idea of what has been said.

The practice of feigning understanding is, of course, not confined to foreign-language speakers. Occasionally we have all pretended to know what was going on when we were, in truth, utterly confused. We usually do this for three reasons:

1. We do not want to appear foolish or ignorant.

2. We do not want to insult the speaker by implying that the material has not been explained well.

3. We are concerned that even if we ask for the material to be repeated, we will not understand it the second time.

It is impossible to maintain an efficiently run workplace unless managers can be certain that their instructions have been understood. The following suggestions will help you assess how much information has actually gotten across.

1. **Watch for nonverbal signs.** Although nonverbal signals can be very helpful in assessing how much has been understood, body language is by no means universal throughout the world. A blank expression may be a sign of poor understanding for most people but in The Far East is more likely to reflect the Asian desire to avoid an overt display of emotion. Similarly, the avoidance of eye contact can indicate that the person is not following you but can also be an indication of respect.

This is not to say that body language is of no use in assessing understanding. It is still fairly safe to assume that when a worker narrows his or her eyes, stays focused on the speaker, and nods and smiles appropriately that he or she is generally grasping what you are saying. Beware, however, of perpetual nodding and smiling that does not relate directly to what you are saying. This behavior might reflect a desire to please and often indicates very little real comprehension.

In Filipino culture there is one nonverbal cue that can be particularly confusing. The Filipino is likely to move the head down as a way of indicating "no." Managers should be careful not to misinterpret this movement as an affirmative nod when asking the question, "Do you understand?"

2. **Notice a lack of interruptions.** Although some people misinterpret this as an indication of attentiveness, a complete lack of interruptions often means that the material is not being understood.

3. **Notice efforts to change the subject.** This could indicate that the listener is not understanding what you are saying so is anxious to talk about something more familiar.

4. **Note the complete absence of questions.** Paradoxically, this often means that the listener is not grasping what you are saying. Perhaps he or she is not understanding enough to allow for the formulation of questions.

5. **Notice inappropriate laughter.** A self-conscious giggle can indicate poor comprehension. Do not interpret laughter as a sign of disrespect for what you are saying. It more likely is a way of covering up embarrassment.

6. **Invite questions in private and in writing.** By providing the opportunity to ask questions in private or in writing, you spare the listener the humiliation of having to admit a lack of understanding in front of colleagues or friends. This suggestion is especially valuable during training sessions when the number of people present can make it particularly difficult for the trainee to admit his or her confusion.

Note: In the training room, loss of face can also be avoided by using self-graded quizzes. Avoid the use of multiple-choice tests when quizzing immigrant workers. Such tools rely too often on a knowledge of English idioms and, therefore, serve to test English-language facility more than course content.

7. **Allow enough time for questions to be formulated.** Remember that nonnative speakers need more time in which to construct questions. A worker who is rushed may miss the opportunity to clear up an important point.

8. **Beware of the "yes" that means "Yes, I hear your question," not "Yes, I understand."** In Asia, it is appropriate to answer any question with an initial "yes." This positive response is often merely an acknowledgment that the question has been heard and understood; it is not an actual answer to a specific inquiry.

9. **Beware of a positive response to a negative question.** In English, when asked, "You don't understand, do you?" the appropriate response, if the listener does not understand, is to say, "No [I do not understand]." In many Asian languages, on the other hand, the way of communicating a negative response would be to say "Yes [I agree with you that I do not understand]."

Remember to phrase all questions in the positive, that is "Do you understand?" rather than, "You don't understand, do you?" If asked a negatively phrased question by an Asian immigrant, answer it with a complete sentence. If you say just "yes" or "no," the meaning of your response could easily be taken as the opposite of what you intended.

10. **Beware of a qualified yes in response to the question, "Do you understand?"** Tentative answers such as "Yes, I think so" and "I suppose so" may be efforts to cushion the abruptness of a negative response and amount to a gentle way of saying "No, I do not understand [but I am not comfortable coming right out and saying so]."

11. **Have the listener repeat what you have said.** This is a simple way of assessing understanding. There are, however, a couple of pitfalls to this approach. First, if at all possible, it must be done in private to avoid loss of face in front of others. Second, you should be skeptical if you get back a word-for-word recitation of what you have just said. Rote repetition may indi-

cate merely the ability to mouth the words, not a real under-standing of the material.

Note: One way around this is to ask workers to solve a problem or perform a demonstration using the information you have just provided. This requires them to show understanding and proves that they have the ability to use your instructions, not just repeat your words.

12. **Observe behavior and inspect production.** If the proce-dure that has been taught is done correctly the first time, the chances are good that your instructions have been understood and that they will continue to be carried out.

When checking for understanding in the office, plant, or training room, it is important to avoid putting the immigrant or ethnic worker in an uncomfortable or conspicuous position. By using the techniques provided here, it is possible to assess how much has been understood while preserving the dignity and pride of the worker.

Understanding Nonnative English Speakers

Now that we have explored ways in which to make ourselves understood and methods for knowing how successful we have been, we are still faced with the challenge of understanding what a nonnative speaker is saying. This is a task that varies in diffi-culty depending on the thickness of the accent, the country of origin, and the manager's own familiarity with a particular accent.

If you are feeling especially frustrated in your ability to un-derstand the accents of your workers, you might be encouraged by this last comment. You will be glad to know that the more you hear a particular accent, the easier it is to understand. Our ears and minds gradually adapt to new sounds and new ways of pronouncing words, and eventually even the thickest accent be-comes easily decipherable. In the meantime, however, there are some techniques that will help you better understand nonnative English speakers.

1. **Share responsibility for poor communication.** If, for example, you speak on the telephone with immigrant workers whom you have difficulty understanding, you might comment from time to time on the bad connection or noise in the room that keeps you from being able to hear clearly. The purpose of a small deception such as this is to take some of the load off the worker who is already self-conscious about his or her accent. The more responsibility you can accept for not understanding, the less pressure employees will be under, and the more relaxed they will be. This relaxation allows the foreign-born worker to focus on pronunciation, speak more slowly, and communicate more successfully.

2. **Invite the speaker to speak more slowly.** It is important for the manager to avoid talking too fast when speaking with the immigrant worker. Speed is also one of the main reasons that foreign accents are difficult to understand. Because we all talk faster when we are uncomfortable, it is important to make the nonnative English speaker as relaxed as possible.

Some immigrants, too, feel that if they speak English rapidly, they will appear more fluent. Although speed certainly does represent a facility with vocabulary and grammar, it can also interfere with the ability to be understood.

3. **Repeat what you believe the immigrant has said.** Saying, for example, "As I understand it, you mean . . . " can be a quick and easy way to establish if you have heard correctly. This habit gives the worker the opportunity to clarify what was meant and gives you a way of communicating the fact that you really care about what the employee has to say.

4. **Encourage the worker to use the written word.** The written word works both ways: it helps you communicate to the worker, and it helps the worker communicate to you. It is, in many cases, not only easier to read English than to hear it but also easier to write it than to speak it. This brings us back to the point that some immigrants have a highly developed knowledge of English vocabulary and grammar but have difficulty with pronunciation. The written word gets around this problem.

5. **Allow the worker to spell difficult words.** Admittedly it can be embarrassing to ask a speaker to spell out what he or she is trying to say. Nonetheless, this technique can substantially

shorten what could be an otherwise long and painful exchange. Spelling is particularly helpful when working with foreign names, some of which are unfamiliar to the native-born manager.

6. **Read the speaker's lips.** We have seen how helpful it is to allow the worker to see the manager's lips in order to understand more easily. This same practice is helpful in the other direction. Looking at the immigrant's lips can be useful in clarifying words that would otherwise be very difficult to decipher.

7. **Give the speaker plenty of time in which to communicate.** Nothing is more rattling than having to hurry. We already know how important it is to give the speaker enough time in which to formulate questions and responses. Create an atmosphere in which the conversation is leisurely and during which there is plenty of room for pauses, for collecting one's thoughts, and for relaxation.

8. **Listen to all that the speaker has to say before assuming that you do not understand.** In this instance, the rules are different for you than for the foreign-language speaker. I have mentioned how important it is for you not to let too much material go by before checking for understanding. In the case of your listening to the foreign-language speaker, it is better to do the opposite: listen to a large amount of what the speaker has to say. Once you have evaluated the individual words and phrases in context, you will have a better understanding.

9. **Observe body language.** Although the vocabulary of nonverbal language varies from culture to culture, it can still provide general clues as to the essence, if not the specifics, of what is being said. The worker who is ringing his or her hands is obviously nervous, and the employee who is grimacing is probably angry or upset. Nonverbal signals such as these tell us far more about the emotions of the speaker than do the words they speak. They also give us clues that help us decipher the meaning behind culturally different ways of expressing ideas. The Asian who does not want to hurt you by stating a definite "no" is likely to soften a negative reply by saying, "Maybe," or "We'll see." If you look carefully, you may notice that as these words are being said, the speaker's head will move down, a negative sign that counteracts the words being spoken.

10. **Remember to listen and expect to understand.** Studies have shown that most of us listen at only 30 percent of capacity and that this percentage drops when we do not expect to understand. When we hear a foreign accent, for example, there is the danger of thinking, "I'll never understand what this person is saying," and then to conclude that there is no point in even trying to understand. The result is that we stop listening. Moreover, when we hear a foreign accent, we tend to listen to the accent rather than to what is being said. Be aware of your listening habits. Are you truly listening to the words, or are you merely focusing on the way those words are pronounced?

Encouraging the Speaking of English

English is a difficult language; it is replete with subtle idioms, words that sound one way and look another (*February*, *psychology*, and *laughter* are the classic examples), and single words with several different meanings. The word *check*, for example, has at least seven meanings, ranging from the bill you receive in a restaurant to the tiny pattern in your suit.

To get some idea of how dangerous it is to speak English, examine these signs authored by proprietors around the world for the benefit of English-speaking tourists. In a Hong Kong tailor shop, women are asked to "have a fit upstairs"; at a hotel in Japan, guests are invited to "take advantage of the chambermaid"; and tourists are met in a Moscow hotel lobby with the greeting, "If this is your first trip to Moscow, you're welcome to it".[1] All of these sentences contain perfect vocabulary and grammar, yet their meaning is certainly not what the proprietors intended.

It is no wonder that immigrant workers are often hesitant to speak up in meetings, to ask questions, or to participate in conversations in English. It is all too easy to make an embarrassing mistake. The fear of humiliation is combined with the concern that, if they begin to speak English, those around them will assume they know more than they do and, consequently, will launch into a long conversation.

These are the reasons that so many workers, even those with a fair grasp of the language, are reluctant to use it. What can you do to overcome these fears and to encourage the speaking of English in the workplace?

1. **Learn a few words of the worker's language.** It may seem like a contradiction to learn the workers' language so they will be motivated to speak more English, but by learning just a few words of the languages found in your workplace, you are showing a respect for the workers' culture, which they will be eager to return.

Perhaps this idea can be better understood if you think of a time when you were in a foreign country and someone made an effort to greet you in your own language. When this happened, you probably felt relieved, respected, and grateful. Possibly you became more willing to try a few words of the host country's language. By communicating this same respect to your foreign-born workers and colleagues, you will be encouraging them to return the favor by speaking more English on the job.

For those concerned that learning just a few words of a language is tokenism and that it is patronizing, remember that a behavior is patronizing only if the manager is acting out of that emotion. If learning to say "good morning" in Korean is motivated by a desire to show friendship and respect, it will serve that purpose. On the other hand, if your attitude is one of talking down to employees, this too will be what is perceived. Like all the other suggestions in this book, it is the manager's attitude that will dictate whether the immigrant worker interprets a given approach as patronizing or as respectful and compassionate.

It may seem like a daunting job to learn even a few words of such unfamiliar tongues as Tagalog, Vietnamese, or Farsi. To help you out, a few phrases have been included in appendix A, along with a phonetic rendering to help you with the pronunciation. Do not worry too much about the pronunciation. If you pronounce a word incorrectly, remember that your mistake will serve to show the worker that it is all right to try a language and to make an error. Your errors, too, will give workers an opportunity to teach you something for a change—a switch in roles that quickly promotes good communication and mutual respect.

Note: You will notice from the list in the appendix that it is important to learn the phrase, "That's all I know," in order to keep from getting lost in a lengthy conversation.

I mentioned above that if you are going to translate material into other languages, you must be certain to include all the languages found in your company. The same applies to the learning of a few words of your workers' languages; just a few phrases of each will prevent any possible resentments or bad feelings.

2. **Smile, look enthusiastic, and be patient.** Use the same techniques you would use when encouraging anyone to speak. Nod your head when appropriate, say encouraging phrases like "I understand" and "go on," and above all else, do not show impatience. If the worker appears embarrassed while attempting English, glance away from time to time. This will help the speaker feel less "in the spotlight," and, therefore, less self-conscious.

Managers are busy; they do not always have time for lengthy conversations or conversations that move along slowly. When communicating with workers who do not speak English well, try to see to it that you do so at times when you will not be tempted to cut the conversation short or hurry it along. We have seen the importance of allowing enough time for pauses and questions—this requires patience, or at least the impression of patience, on the manager's part.

3. **Ask open-ended questions.** There is a temptation when speaking with those whose English is not highly developed to ask "yes" and "no" questions. We do this because it gives us the comforting illusion that we are having a successful two-way conversation. The truth, however, is that a "yes" or "no" answer can be misleading. In addition, giving workers the option of answering just "yes" or "no" discourages them from supplying a lengthier answer.

Should you wish, for example, to find out how a worker

feels about his or her job, you would be better off inquiring, "Tell me about your job," than saying, "Do you like your job?" or even, "How is your job?" Both of these latter queries allow the worker to answer with a brief "yes" or "no" or, equally unrevealing, "fine." Similarly, "Tell me your ideas," is better than "Have you any ideas?"

When you phrase questions, see to it that they encourage and even demand more conversation. Not only will the worker have the opportunity to voice more ideas and practice more English, but you will get the chance to know that worker better and to assess how much English he or she can speak and understand.

4. **Ask a series of short questions to keep the conversation going.** You may have noticed that some workers will answer a question and then be silent, in contrast to many native-born or highly assimilated employees who will continue to talk as a way of showing how bright and enthusiastic they are. Whether the immigrant worker is falling silent out of respect for authority or because of a fear of speaking English, you can remedy the situation by asking a series of questions. Structure these questions so that they demand more than a one-word answer, and you will facilitate a more successful two-way exchange.

5. **Do not laugh at workers' English, even if they do.** Sometimes when people laugh at themselves, we get the impression that it is all right for others to laugh as well. In the case of employees who are struggling to speak English and making the occasional error in pronunciation or usage, it is best to assume that they would not appreciate even your good-natured laughter. Language facility is a personal matter; it is one thing for a worker to laugh at himself or herself and quite another to be teased by a superior.

6. **Positively reinforce good communication.** In the next chapter, we will see that excessive praise of some immigrant employees is not always the most effective way to motivate desired behaviors. Nevertheless, it is important to notice when a worker is trying to speak English and to praise that effort quietly.

Summary

We have come a long way from the days when the founding fathers wondered how to cope with a relatively small influx of German-speaking immigrants. Language diversity has come to be one of the greatest challenges facing management today. Yet having access to workers who speak more than one language is a significant asset in our shrinking world. The information in this chapter, whose key points are summarized below, will help managers and human-resource professionals minimize the challenges while maximizing use of these valuable employees.

- Understand the immigrant worker's perspective.
- Do not jump to conclusions about what undeveloped English-language facility means.
- Speak slowly, distinctly, and simply, and be concrete.
- Use familiar words and avoid jargon, slang, and idioms.
- Allow pauses, do not talk too much, and be organized.
- Use and observe body language and tone of voice (cautiously).
- Use the written word.
- Utilize group leaders.
- Recap and check for understanding frequently.
- Avoid embarrassing the immigrant worker when assessing for understanding.
- Share responsibility for mutual communication.
- Learn a few words of their language.
- Listen carefully.
- EXPECT TO SUCCEED!

Note

1. Verbal communication, "The Ken and Bob Company," KABC Radio, Los Angeles.

3
A Different Perspective
Bridging the Value Gap

By knowing the language of a culture, you know its voice—by
knowing its values, you know its heart.

—Anonymous

This chapter covers:

- The definition and function of values
- The impact of the value placed on avoiding negative confrontations
- The importance of saving face
- The impact of the desire for personal anonymity
- The value some groups place on the group over the individual
- The importance of building well-rounded relationships
- The role of informal group leaders
- Varying attitudes toward authority

The Challenge

Arthur Edwards is suffering from culture shock. No, he is
not some wholesome, ruddy-cheeked farm boy stuck in
the shifting sands of exotic Saudi Arabia nor a mellow
southerner attempting to fit into the bustle of downtown
Tokyo. Arthur is in shock much closer to home: right in
California where he is a high-level manager at a large

computer firm in the Silicon Valley. There are days, however when Arthur feels as if he were in Southeast Asia.
The electronics industry is full of Vietnamese workers, and Arthur's firm is no exception. Arthur used to
enjoy working with his courteous, precise, and hard-
working Vietnamese staff. Despite a bit of difficulty with
the language, Arthur prided himself on communicating effectively, and, although his relationship with
the workers was a bit formal, he was encouraged
when employees inevitably smiled when he entered the
plant.

In response to this sign of friendliness, Arthur tried to
establish a comfortable and casual working environment.
He invited the staff to use his first name, rolled up his
sleeves and worked alongside them, and ate his lunch in
the employees' cafeteria.

Unfortunately, his well-intended efforts backfired. After the changes, the staff seemed distant and reserved, not
more content as Arthur had expected. Worse, one of the
older, more experienced workers resigned without expla-
nation.

Arthur felt like a failure—inadequate, disoriented, angry, and frustrated. His customary behaviors—his culturally rooted desire to create warmth and loyalty by being
informal—had not had the effect he anticipated when
applied to another culture. For Arthur the situation was
particularly distressing because he was working on his
home territory. He was not accustomed to thinking in
terms of cultural diversity as he might have had he been
manufacturing the same computers with a Japanese staff
in Japan.

Arthur's feelings of inadequacy and disorientation represent a
classic case of culture shock. As we saw in chapter 1, culture
shock occurs when one's usual behaviors do not elicit the expected reaction. In this instance, Arthur was trying to achieve a
response—greater warmth and closeness—by using an American
value—informality and social equality—within a cultural group

that is far more comfortable with formal relationships and permanent hierarchies of authority.

The inadequacy Arthur felt and the obvious discomfort his staff experienced could easily have been avoided. The situation would have been greatly improved had Arthur been more experienced in the ways of cross-cultural communication and, in this case, in the differences in culturally based values between foreign-born employees and American management.

What Are Values?

Values form the core of culture. It is from values that other elements of culture arise; etiquette, life-style, and even language are shaped by the values of a society. Values tell us what to care about, what to strive for, and how to behave; they range from notions of how to treat the boss to how much education is important.

Some values are consistent among cultures. Few would deny, for example, that the desires for physical comfort and human companionship are universal. Other values are, if not unique to one people, at least ranked differently in their hierarchy of concerns. The American value of self-reliance and independence from the family is, for example, highly treasured here but is considered to be a low priority in the Middle East or Asia.

Ideas about the importance of anticipating and controlling the future vary significantly from culture to culture. Whereas the native-born or assimilated American worker would place a high priority on planning for retirement, accumulating sick days, and purchasing insurance, the immigrant worker might be more concerned with meeting today's obligations and enjoying the present moment. These and other value differences can have a profound impact on how diverse workers are managed and on how cooperation and teamwork are achieved.

Why Learn about Cultural Values?

Why is it so important to study culturally diverse values, especially if we cannot be certain that all members of a particular group share the same values? The reason is that values affect the workplace and the behavior of workers in four important ways:

1. **Values dictate felt needs.** Managers cannot accurately assess the needs and expectations of employees without first understanding their culturally specific values. Without this understanding of needs and desires, efforts to motivate productivity and cooperation can be seriously impaired.

2. **Values dictate what is defined as a problem.** An Asian employee might feel good about his or her tendency not to complain when dissatisfied or to ask questions when confused. The American manager, on the other hand, may see these behaviors as problems reflecting a lack of openness and an unwillingness to learn.

3. **Values dictate how problems are solved.** A Filipino worker might solve an interpersonal conflict by asking for a transfer to another department in an effort to avoid the loss of harmony that would result from a direct confrontation. A native-born colleague could regard this solution as possibly cowardly and evasive, preferring instead to deal, in typical American fashion, with the problem directly.

4. **Values dictate expectations of behavior.** Hispanic workers will expect the manager to take time to chat and get to know them as human beings—to learn about their families, home lives, and interests. To behave differently can leave workers with an impression of coldness, which is not conducive to the building of productive, harmonious relationships.

Values must be understood if managers are to work effectively with immigrant and ethnic workers. The values discussed in this chapter are central to that understanding. Some of these ideas are so important that many of them turn up repeatedly throughout this book where their specific applications to successful cross-cultural management are explored.

Understanding Values

Harmony and Balance

The desire for harmony and balance in all social and professional situations is a value held throughout most of the non-Western world. Although based on a broad philosophical principle and rooted in both medicine and religion, this notion has specific, and significant, applications for the development of effective cross-cultural business relationships. Cultures that place great importance on harmony and balance maintain these values in three essential ways:

1. By avoiding direct or negative confrontations

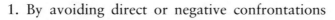

2. By minimizing embarrassment to all participants in an interaction; that is, by saving face for all concerned

3. By not calling attention to the individual at the expense of the group

With a little practice, each of these can be recognized and understood so as to facilitate communication and minimize misunderstandings.

Avoiding Negative Confrontations. The value placed on avoiding negative confrontations is quite alien to mainstream American thinking. Expressed in Filipino culture by the term *pakikisama* ("smooth human relationships"), the desire to soften directly negative statements is common to many cultures throughout the world. This value is difficult for most Americans to grasp because for us "telling it like it is" is an ideal toward which everyone should strive.

Numerous American phrases, idioms, and proverbs reflect this desire for truth at all cost. Exercise 3–1 is useful in helping you and your managers become more aware of how much this perspective permeates American society. See how many phrases or proverbs you can think of that express this value. The list has been primed with two examples to get you started.

Exercise 3–1. Expressing Truth at Any Cost

1. "Would you please get to the point."

2. "Honesty is the best policy."

3.

4.

5.

6.

7.

8.

9.

10.

I could trace for pages the historical roots of this "tell-it-like-it-is," "straight talk" mentality, but our concern here is not so much the why of it but the how: how can managers deal with the often crippling confusion that results when two diametrically opposed values come into contact? The following dialogue between Andy, a supervisor at a large manufacturing company, and Juan, one of his best Mexican workers, illustrates the kinds of problems that can arise.

Dialogue	Speaker's Thoughts
Andy: Juan, will the trucks be loaded by five o'clock?	*Andy*: (They'd better be. This is an important delivery.)[a]
Juan: Don't worry, they'll be ready in plenty of time.[b]	*Juan*: (We are short of workers today, I hope we can make it.)[c]

(Andy returns to find the trucks only partly loaded.)

Dialogue	Speaker's Thoughts
Andy: What happened? You said the job would be done on time?[d]	*Andy*: (Juan has let me down. He has either lied to me or misjudged how long the job would take.)[e]
Juan: (looking away) I'm sorry. We did the best we could.[f]	*Juan*: (Why is he so angry? He knows we are working hard. Besides, I was only trying to spare him worry.)[g]
	Andy: (Juan is so shifty, he doesn't look at me and won't even defend himself.)[h]

What went wrong? Let us examine each element to see the misunderstandings illustrated here and how they might have been avoided:

Element a: Precise scheduling is of great importance in the United States but much less so in Hispanic countries. We will look at the issue of time and punctuality again in the discussion of cultural variations in etiquette.

Elements b and c: These elements reflect Juan's concern that the job may not be completed on time but also his worry that if he states his doubts directly to the boss, negative feelings and conflict might be created. He is also concerned that if he speaks negatively to the boss, he will be showing disrespect to an authority figure. This attitude is common not only with Hispanic workers but with Asian employees as well. Even Shakespeare might have agreed with Juan when he said, "Though it be honest, it is never good to bring bad news."

Juan is not lying. He is doing what he believes to be proper and compassionate: sparing the boss's feelings and thereby maintaining a good relationship.

American culture is not devoid of behaviors designed to avoid confrontation. "Let's have lunch," "See you later," and "I'll call you soon" are frequently nothing more than polite ways of ending a conversation when a speaker has no real intention of seeing the other person again. Statements like these are not considered lies, only gracious evasions. We are likely to comment on a poor "nice dinner" or even to say, "Don't call us, we'll call you," without considering ourselves guilty of any real dishonesty.

Elements d and e: Since Andy is unaware of the Hispanic desire to avoid directly negative statements, he draws the only conclusion he can: that Juan is either deliberately lying or is incompetent at his job.

Element f: Juan's first instinct is to look away from his boss in order to communicate respect and regret that the job has not worked out well. He does not, however, launch into a litany of apology, for that would serve to heighten the confrontation and disrupt the balance by calling attention to himself.

Element g: Juan's thoughts illustrate the importance of mutual cultural understanding between workers and management. If Juan had known of the importance of informing Andy of the time constraints, he would probably have realized that he was not helping his boss by keeping the truth from him. If Andy had understood Juan's perspective, he might have been less angry and more able to resolve the situation constructively.

Element h: In American culture, lack of eye contact is considered a sign of dishonesty, not respect. Andy assumes, particularly because Juan does not defend himself, that he is indeed dishonest.

This dialogue reflects only one aspect of the desire to avoid direct confrontations: the hesitance to tell others, especially authority figures, of bad news. Other manifestations of this same value include the Asian practice of saying "no" in an indirect fashion and the reluctance of some workers to complain about problems in the workplace.

This latter behavior may seem like a blessing. Perhaps you are thinking how lovely it would be if employees stopped complaining about poor relationships, inadequate equipment, or undesirable working conditions. The problem with this fantasy is that if you are not informed of difficulties in the workplace, there is no way that they can be resolved.

Asian workers in particular are likely to state complaints in such discrete terms that they become almost unrecognizable. The classic joke concerning this behavior involves the Japanese gentleman whose foot is being stepped on by an American. Rather than abruptly ask the American to move, the Japanese man genteelly comments, "My foot is under yours." This approach to the problem is very different from that found in mainstream American culture where speaking up for oneself is a virtue and where "the squeaky wheel gets the grease."

The following dilemma explores some possible solutions to the difficulties created when a worker refuses to complain about a problem in the workplace. Readers are provided with a choice of responses to a specific situation. Choose the response you think best.

> A usually outgoing and cheerful Filipino worker has recently become rather withdrawn and quiet on the job. You have heard rumors that she is upset because another worker has been hostile toward her, but she refuses to complain or even talk about the incident. How would you handle the situation?
>
> a. I would assume that the worker has a personal reason for keeping the problem to herself and would not intrude. Eventually she will work it out or get over it.
>
> b. I would tell the employee that she is overreacting.
>
> c. I would ask fellow workers what the trouble might be.

> d. I would gently explain to the employee that in order for me to do a good job, I need her to keep me informed of any difficulties.

Now it is time to evaluate the options:

a. Of course, it is possible that the employee has personal reasons for keeping the problem a secret. Because of her cultural background, however, it is safer to assume that the Filipino value of not complaining to superiors is at play here. This wait-and-see attitude could cost you an opportunity to build a better, more open relationship with this woman.

b. As a last resort, this approach might work with a native-born American who values a direct approach, but for most immigrant workers, this attitudes would be taken as patronizing, insulting, and even cruel.

c. This might be a solution, but be careful not to betray any confidences. Hispanics and Asians in particular value discretion and would not wish for other employees to know of their difficulty. This is one reason that they generally prefer resolving conflicts in private.

d. *Good answer!* As we shall see shortly, many foreign-born workers place great importance on preserving the dignity and meeting the needs of those around them. This approach calls on this value by inviting the worker to help you do a better job. In short, you are finding the correct fit between the worker's values and your own needs.

Throughout this book, you will encounter other examples of this desire to avoid direct confrontation. Managers need to bear in mind that although this behavior can seem bewildering and frustrating, it usually arises out of a gracious desire to sustain harmonious relationships.

Saving Face. The Chinese have a proverb: "If you disregard the question of face, life is pointless." Saving face is a concept frequently misunderstood in the West. This value, which lies at the heart of the desire to maintain harmony and balance, involves the notion that none of the parties in a relationship or situation should suffer embarrassment. A Korean, for example, who is passed over for promotion in favor of a younger countryman, will suffer serious loss of *kibun* ("face") and is likely to quit rather than endure what is experienced as profound humiliation. The Filipino worker may suffer what is known as *hiya* ("shame") should a suggestion for improvement be offered insensitively and therefore be taken as an insult.

American culture puts nowhere near the emphasis on saving face as do most other cultures. Native-born Americans are more prepared to risk embarrassment, especially if the result of such a risk is perceived of as worthwhile.

The desire to save face is manifested in a number of behaviors, each of which can have a profound impact on the success of personal and professional relationships and each of which reflects a different concern. Table 3–1 lists these behaviors and the central fears associated with each.

The following situations will help you and your managers discover how to interpret these various behaviors. They provide specific examples in which saving face is the central issue. Each case is followed by a selection of possible interventions. Identify the response you feel is best while remembering that there may

Table 3–1
Saving Face

Behavior	Concern or Fear
A reluctance to admit lack of understanding or to ask questions	Appearing ignorant
A reluctance to take the initiative on tasks or to perform a task in a new way	Doing the task wrong and appearing foolish or losing one's job
A tendency to avoid stating a definite refusal although that is the intended meaning	Causing the other party to feel at a disadvantage and therefore experience loss of face
A dislike for public criticism	Being embarrassed in front of others
A tendency to avoid asking for promotions	Humiliation if turned down

be more than one correct answer to each dilemma. Evaluations of the options follow each example.

Situation 1—The Training Room: When workers who have emigrated from Mexico fail to ask questions in the training room, I:

a. Assume they understand the information and proceed on that basis

b. Am careful to repeat the material again because I realize that the workers may not understand but are reluctant to say so because of fear of embarrassment

c. Recognize that the workers may not understand but feel that it is their responsibility to speak up and ask questions

d. Ask the informal leaders of the group to ask questions in class so that the others will understand that it is acceptable to do so

Evaluating the Options

a. You could be correct in this assumption; on the other hand, you could be wrong. What is at risk, for you and for the worker, is a task efficiently and properly completed.

b. *This is a good answer.* What is there to lose except maybe a few moments? Admittedly it can be irritating when a worker does not admit a lack of understanding, but it is important to realize that American culture values inquisitiveness; students are taught to ask questions at an early age. In many other countries, though, asking questions is considered not only embarrassing but also rude and disrespectful in that it implies that the trainer has not done a complete job.

c. This answer may conform to the American emphasis on personal responsibility, but a hard-nosed attitude like this can only prove counterproductive for all concerned.

d. *This is an excellent answer.* As we saw in the discussion of language differences, informal group leaders are often valuable resources for manager and trainer alike. Not only might you ask the leaders to model the desired behavior but also to tell the others that you would like them to ask questions in class.

Situation 2—Taking the Initiative: When a foreign-born employee fails to take the initiative on a task, I usually:

   a. Assume that he or she is lacking in self-esteem and recommend counseling

   b. Say that he or she will be penalized if it happens again

   c. Explain to the employee that taking the initiative is valued in the American corporation and that it is all right to learn from one's mistakes

   d. Enter into a pact with the employee that if he or she makes an error when taking the initiative, I promise not to get angry but to praise him or her for being willing to take a chance

Evaluating the Options

a. This is possible but unlikely. Probably the employee is a well-adjusted person who is acting the way his or her culture dictates.

b. Although many foreign-born workers are accustomed to an authoritarian boss, penalizing a behavior rooted in cultural misunderstanding will be unproductive.

c. *Good answer!* As we will see in the chapter on motivation, providing information about American culture is an important but often overlooked first step to successful cross-cultural management.

d. *This is another good answer.* It directly addresses cultural differences and includes both the manager and the worker in the solution.

Situation 3—Cross-Cultural Criticism: When it is necessary to criticize an employee, I am careful to:

a. Do so in front of other workers so they too will learn what not to do

b. State the criticism as a mutual problem rather than as an attack

c. State the problem forcefully while honestly sharing my feelings of anger

d. Pad criticism with positive statements like, "Your work in other areas is very good "

Evaluating the Options

a. This is a poor option. Loss of face, feelings of shame, and embarrassment are worse for everyone when experienced in front of others. You probably remember how upset you were in grade school when the teacher criticized you in front of your friends in order to make an example. Middle-Eastern and Asian workers are particularly sensitive to this treatment.

b. *This is a good idea.* By deflecting attention from the individual, there is less chance of his or her feeling personally threatened and diminished. As we shall see in chapter 5, a sense of psychological safety is one of the most important components of motivation and behavior change.

c. Venting one's anger in a management situation is rarely productive, and even less so when the anger is directed at an immigrant worker who, although probably accustomed to an authoritarian boss, expects to be treated with fairness and paternalism. Also remember that Asian cultures regard excessive displays of emotion as improper and diminishing of respect and that Hispanic workers are quick to lose respect for a boss who loses his or her temper.

d. *Positive reinforcement is always the right answer.* By padding criticism with positive statements, you provide the worker with the psychological room in which to hear and be receptive to less positive comments. The trick is to know when to stop. Whereas Middle Eastern workers are comfortable with giving and receiving compliments, Asians are ill at ease with excess praise and are at times even skeptical of it. Be alert to these feelings and issue your compliments with sincerity and restraint.

We all want dignity. Each culture achieves this in a different way. For the native-born American or those who have been assimilated, this need may be met through hard work, independence, patriotism, or the achievement of financial security. For many other cultures, dignity lies in the preservation of what the Greeks call *philotimo* ("self-respect," "honor") or what the Filipinos term *amor propio*—a Spanish phrase which means "self-worth." Preserving the *amor propio* of staff and colleagues is one of the most important steps that any manager can take toward building a more effective multicultural workplace.

Not Calling Attention to the Individual. The Japanese proverb that reads, "The nail that sticks out gets hammered down," illustrates another manifestation of the desire for harmony and balance. In sharp contrast to the American value of honoring and distinguishing the individual, this perspective holds that every effort must be made to maintain anonymity within a group. The following dialogue focuses on one of the most common situations in which this desire for anonymity is likely to be encountered.

Woo has come to a large company to interview for a supervisory position for which he is very qualified and which he wants very much. Krista, the human-resource director, is pleased with his application.

Dialogue	*Speaker's Thoughts*
Krista: Your schooling and work history are very impressive. What else can you tell me about your qualifications for the job?[a]	*Krista*: (This fellow is perfect. I'm eager to hear how he presents himself.)[b]
Woo: Well, I don't know. I'd just like to work for your company.[c]	*Woo*: (Why is she asking me? It's all on the application. I don't want to brag.)[d]
	Krista: (He sure is lacking in confidence. I wonder what that means for his ability to perform. Also, he doesn't seem to want the job very much. His background is so good, though, I'll give him a chance.)[e]

Krista hires Woo. He does such a good job that in six months he is being considered for a higher position. Yet despite his awareness of the new opening, Woo does not apply for the job.

Krista: Why haven't you applied for this higher position?[f]	*Krista*: (He is so unassertive or maybe he's lazy. Doesn't he care? This passive behavior does not fit with Woo's obvious love of his work.)[g]
Woo: I haven't applied because I feel that if the company wanted me for the job, you would offer it to me.[h]	*Woo*: (This is so strange. Don't they know what they want? It's not my place to ask for a higher position. My work speaks for itself.)[i]

Does Woo have an emotional problem? Is he lacking in self-esteem, confidence, and self-interest? Probably not. The following analysis indicates that a behavior that might be interpreted as neurotic in the context of one culture will appear normal when evaluated in the context of the culture in which the behavior was taught.

Elements a and b: According to American business etiquette, it is desirable to speak up regarding one's achievements and qualifications.

Elements c and d: Woo does not understand why he is being put in the awkward position of having to sing his own praises. In Chinese culture, it is considered offensive and disharmonious to brag and show off in a situation such as this. This applies as well to most other Asian nations, to native American cultures, and, to a lesser extent, to most Hispanic cultures.

Note: In many countries, jobs are acquired through family loyalty or personal affiliation, not through qualifications. In those cases, the issue of praising oneself never arises.

This desire not to "show off" is also manifested in the conference or training room where some immigrant and ethnic workers are hesitant to voice innovative ideas out of a concern of appearing arrogant and calling inordinate attention to themselves.

Element e: Krista, because of her American background, does not understand Woo's reticence but instinctively knows he is right for the job. This is one of the many cases in which managers of multicultural work forces can and should rely on their instincts and experience when making decisions.

Elements f and g: Krista does not realize that the Western value of always striving for a higher position is not universal. Some foreign-born and ethnic workers do not seek promotions because they feel that the new position will disrupt harmony by calling attention to themselves as individuals. This does not mean that managers should overlook these workers, but merely that they will often need to be sought out and encouraged to apply.

Elements h and i: Woo considers it the responsibility of his superior to choose him for promotion. His goal, like that of many other immigrant workers, is to work for the good of the company, not for his own benefit.

There is another reason that Woo might be hesitant to seek this promotion aggressively. He knows that in doing so he is risking a serious loss of face should he be turned down, a humiliation that might necessitate his resigning in order to redress the balance.

Minimizing one's skills during an interview and not aggressively going after a promotion reflect the value placed on not calling attention to the individual. Perhaps the most dramatic example of this attitude is seen in Lebanon, where prospective employees bring along a companion to present the applicant's qualifications. In this way, the applicant does not have to suffer the embarrassment of doing so for himself or herself. In other parts of the Middle East, however, self-praise is expected. Be careful not to generalize.

The Group over the Individual

Closely related to the issue of harmony and balance is the value of putting the individual second to the family or the group. In most of the world, the needs of the family, community, and even corporation come before those of any one person. "The hand of God is with the group" is an Arab proverb that illustrates this perspective. Loyalty in the Hispanic community goes first to God, then to the family, and finally to the individual. In Japan, Americans are frequently surprised to hear a Japanese colleague use the plural when referring to a successfully completed task— "we did it"—even if the accomplishment was an individual effort.

This prioritizing of family and group runs contrary to many American values and can lead to confusion in the multicultural workplace. The issues summarized in the following pages that look at individual versus group priority are perhaps best exemplified by the curious fact that English is the only major language in which the pronoun *I* is capitalized; the individual and his or her needs and achievements are clearly supreme.

Making Mistakes

The American Perspective. A worker's mistakes are important primarily because they make the individual look bad; any shame brought on the group is a secondary consideration.

The Perspective of Other Cultures. In most cultures, distress over a mistake arises from how the error will affect the group, not how it will reflect on the individual. This concern with group shame is most pronounced in Middle Eastern cultures, followed closely by Hispanic and Asian groups.

Implications. One of the implications of this difference in priorities is the tendency for some workers to be reluctant to take the initiative on tasks or to voice ideas openly. In this case, their concern would be that they might make an error that would reflect on the abilities of the group. On the positive side of this issue, concern with the reputation of the group results in hard and conscientious work designed to ensure that colleagues and superiors evaluate the group favorably.

Finding One's Identity

The American Perspective. A person's identity is determined by individual achievement, not by familial, geographic, or group affiliation.

The Perspective of Other Cultures. In Japan and Mexico, social and geographic links are all important. The Japanese have a term for this; *kankei*, roughly translated, means "human relations" in the sense of a bonding between people from the same locality or company. This common loyalty is clearly seen when one Japanese asks another not "What do you do?" but "Whom do you work for?" By contrast, in the United States, the question would be "What do you do?" with the specific employer being of secondary interest.

Implications. In Mexico, being part of a company means being part of a family. For this reason, firing a person has serious implications and is to be avoided. This fact can create problems for managers of Mexican workers in the United States who are not accustomed to the sometimes casual way in which work forces are disbanded.

Managers might also notice a tendency for workers not to seek promotions if to do so would separate them from the cultural group that generates their identity. Cases have even been reported in which individuals have been asked to be demoted so as to sustain group solidarity. The importance of the family is reflected in how readily many immigrant workers respond to inquiries after family welfare and to the manager who remembers specific family names and events.

Assigning Responsibility

The American Perspective. "The buck stops here": ultimately one person is responsible for a success or failure. Although teamwork is often touted in America, there usually is one hero or one villain associated with all efforts.

The Perspective of Other Cultures. Group responsibility is far more common throughout the rest of the world. As we saw in the discussion of the value placed on harmony and balance, it is in poor taste to call attention to the achievements of the individual; it is the group that counts.

Implications. This group responsibility can prove frustrating for the American manager who, when faced with a situation, wants to find one person to blame, consult, or praise. Although the temptation to do so is very strong, it must be said that to single out an individual for responsibility is likely to make an adversary out of that person and to damage one's relations with the entire group.

When it is necessary to criticize the performance of a worker, it is sometimes wiser to criticize the group as whole than to pick out the one individual responsible. Similarly many immigrant and ethnic workers will respond more favorably to group praise than to the issuing of individual accolades. This is particularly true of Asian workers, who are uncomfortable having attention drawn to just one person.

The Meaning of Competition

The American Perspective. Competition within a group promotes creativity and productivity.

The Perspective of Other Cultures. Competition among individual members of a group is disruptive to productivity as well as to harmony. The group should work as a whole and for the glory of the whole.

Implications. When supervising culturally diverse workers, managers have often tried to increase productivity by encouraging competition. In most cases, the result has been decreased efficiency and reduced morale. Managers would do better to promote group pride rather than disrupt the group in the name of individual achievement. Offering a trip, for example, as an incentive to individuals may not be effective because only one person in the group stands to benefit from the reward. This same reluctance to compete is found in the meeting and training room, where voicing one's own ideas or answering questions creatively is considered rude and harmful to group solidarity.

Setting Goals

The American Perspective. The goals and desires of the individual are of paramount importance. For the group—whether family or corporation—to interfere with these goals is considered authoritarian and even morally wrong.

The Perspective of Other Cultures. In most of the world, the goals of the family or company come first. For the individual to place his or her desires above the group is to be selfish and inconsiderate.

Implications. The manager will see this point of view reflected in the individual worker's willingness to forgo personal advancement if he or she feels that such a promotion does not fit with the goals of the company at large. It is imperative that management remember that such an attitude by no means connotes low self-esteem or lack of assertiveness.

Achieving Independence

The American Perspective. Independence from the family is desirable. To remain dependent on the nuclear or extended family unit into adulthood is often considered a sign of neuroses. Eddie Rickenbacker, an American hero and World War I flying ace, said that one of the four cornerstones of character in the United States is independence of the individual. It is a sign of effective parenting to have one's children grow up to live largely separate lives.

The Perspective of Other Cultures. To set up a life entirely separate from the family is a sign of irresponsibility and even betrayal. In adulthood, offspring owe allegiance, maybe support, and certainly affection to parents and extended family members.

Implications. Managers must be prepared to work with employees who wish to take extensive time off for family events or to return to the homeland for holidays and other special occasions. They must also be aware that promotions that leave less time for relatives and spouses or that result in decreased opportunity for overtime income—income needed to send home to family members—are likely to be looked upon as undesirable and, will, consequently, be resisted.

Obviously there are many other manifestations of this value of placing the group's needs, goals, and reputation over the desires of the individual. One of these that has not been mentioned, primarily because the topic lies outside the purview of this book, is the issue of the separate national identities that many immigrant and ethnic groups have and that management is often tempted to ignore. Vietnamese, Cambodians, and Laotians, for example, regard themselves as distinct entities and in some cases carry old animosities that can interfere with their ability to work together in harmony.

How attitudes like this are handled in the workplace depends entirely on the specific situation. Whether you mix the groups or put a supervisor from one group over members of another is up to your own judgment and observation. The issue is brought up here merely as a reminder that we need to be sensitive to the historical relationships that many groups have had to each other and to recognize that these relationships can affect the dynamics of the workplace.

Valuing the Whole Person

One of the great charms of the American personality is the ability to make friends quickly and to do so on fairly little evidence of interests held in common. This inclination to make and act on snap judgments is reflected in many aspects of our personal and professional lives.

One way to interpret the behaviors of others accurately is to understand one's own cultural perspective. Exercise 3–2 on page 102 is designed to help you do that by assessing how much you conform to this American value of developing trusting, and even caring, relationships with little exploration into a new acquaintance's background or interests. Circle the number that best indicates the degree of agreement with either statement in the pair: *1* if you strongly agree with the statement on the left; *2* if you agree with the statement on the left; *3* if you agree with the statement on the right; and *4* if you strongly agree with the statement on the right.

If you want to see how "American" you and your managers are in regard to this issue, add up all the numbers you circle

Exercise 3–2. Self-Assessment: Forming Relationships

1. Friendships can be made fairly quickly on the basis of superficial knowledge and instinct.

   1 2 3 4

   Friendships last a lifetime so should be entered into only after careful investigation.

2. Successful hiring decisions can be made based primarily on the applicant's professional qualifications.

   1 2 3 4

   It is necessary to know all about a person—not just professional qualifications—before making a decision.

3. Bosses are respected because of fairness and job skills. The rest of their personalities, hobbies, talents, or social connections are of little importance.

   1 2 3 4

   Respect for superiors is based not only on fairness and skill but also on social connections and talents not directly applicable to the job.

4. To criticize a person's work does not usually reflect on the person as a whole.

   1 2 3 4

   To criticize a person's work is to criticize his or her whole being.

and divide the total by 4. This will give you an average figure. If your average is 2.5 or below, you are very mainstream American in your thinking; the lower the number is, the less concerned you are with evaluating the whole person in a professional or personal relationship. A score higher than 2.5 reveals a concern with more holistic business relationships similar to those fostered in such countries as Japan, Korea, and Mexico.

The statements in exercise 3–2 focus on the central question of how important, or unimportant, it is to form well-rounded personal relationships in the workplace. Statement 1, for example, points to the arguably sad reality that in the United States friendships tend to be formed quickly, to be based on fairly superficial associations, and to be dissolved just as fast. Outside the United States, friendships are not formed until the relationship has been slowly and systematically cemented.

In this connection, work is not considered to be separate from social life. Whereas in the United States friendships are compartmentalized—"work friends" at work, for example, or "church friends" in church—elsewhere a friend is part of all aspects of one's life, with no separation or compartmentalization.

Statement 2 deals with the fact that in the United States we tend to hire not a whole person complete with loyalties, peripheral talents, and personality traits but simply a skill or set of achievements. This hiring mode stems from the American value of evaluating people on the basis of their external achievements rather than according to more internal values and traits.

In the Middle East, by contrast, employees are hired because of their social behavior, loyalty, and likableness, as well as because of their professional achievements. The question is likely to be asked, "Would it please God to give this applicant the job?" In Japan, individuals are hired because of the overall package they represent. The package might include, as an important component, any past associations the applicant has had with key personnel of the corporation—having attended the same school, grown up in the same neighborhood, or belonged to the same organizations, for example. Known as *jinmaku*, this cult of personal connections can be vital to the success of any business relationship.

When hiring foreign-born workers, personnel managers and human-resource directors must be alert to the fact that our insistence on obtaining concrete information regarding schooling, skills, and past experience can appear rude, intrusive, and even cold. This information must be obtained, but if the interviewer takes a few minutes to socialize with the applicants and get to know them, these future employees will feel far more comfortable. Inquiring after a Hispanic or Middle Eastern worker's family is an effective way to show interest, communicate respect, and launch a potentially cooperative and productive relationship. In the case of Middle Eastern males, however, be cautious when asking about female members of the family. In some cases, this can be offensive and be misunderstood.

Statement 3 extends this holistic approach to the boss or manager within a corporation. In the United States, we tend to hide our non-job-related achievements, especially if they seem artistic or academic. Quite the contrary is true in countries like Germany or Mexico, where the mention of such accomplishments generates considerable respect from both colleagues and employees. Reveal your achievements—degrees, talents, publications—to the foreign-born staff, and you, and your managers, will gain respect and admiration.

Statement 4 addresses one of the basic issues of cross-cultural criticism: how to discipline across cultural lines without bringing about alienation. In most of the world, an employee's feeling of self-worth is closely tied to job performance. To criticize, for example, an Iranian's work is to be gravely offensive and to bring insult to the employee as a human being. In short, work and the worker are not compartmentalized.

Managers know that one rule of constructive criticism is to criticize the action, not the person. This principle is all the more important when counseling and disciplining the foreign-born worker. In addition, it is imperative that managers are certain to praise the positive aspects of the employee's efforts to avoid alienation and a breakdown in communication.

Americans are inclined to rush: to be concerned with deadlines, efficiency, and rapid progress. To the foreign-born and ethnic worker, this attitude can appear rude, pushy, and disrespectful. By taking the time to form well-rounded relationships, the American manager can substantially increase cooperation in the multicultural workplace. Remember, too, that relationships for many foreign-born workers are lifelong. Making the effort to get to know a person can result in years of loyalty and productivity.

Attitudes toward Authority

All cultures have authority figures. What varies from group to group are ideas of who these leaders are, what their powers should be, and how they are to be treated. For our purposes, we need to explore two groups of authority figures: informal leaders within ethnic and immigrant groups, and managers in the culturally diverse workplace.

Ethnic and Immigrant Group Leaders. Informal group leaders are found even in American culture in the form of "the most popular kid in school" and the individual who, for example, takes the initiative in organizing activities and community efforts. Among ethnic and immigrant groups this leadership role can take on a far more powerful dimension.

This should not be surprising, for the group and its hierarchy is of paramount importance in many parts of the world. Managers need to be aware of the reality and significance of this hierarchy if they are to communicate effectively with culturally diverse workers and with their informal leadership.

We have examined, for example, the reluctance of some workers to complain about problems in the workplace. Among Hispanic workers, this hesitancy is often resolved through the practice of pooling complaints and having them brought to management by a group leader. When this happens, it is important that managers not judge this action as hostile or cowardly but as merely a culturally specific way of coping with the difficulty.

Although there are no absolute rules by which to assertain the identity of these informal group leaders, here are some guidelines which can help. For one thing, although age may no longer be a guarantee of respect in American culture, it is still considered important in many immigrant and ethnic communities. For this reason, the informal leaders within these groups are often the eldest but not necessarily the most accomplished or senior on the job.

Sometimes the leader is an individual who had a particulary prestigious or powerful role in the past or currently serves a specific function. Among Southeast Asians or Central Americans, for example, this person might be a former military officer or an important figure from the homeland. Often, but not always, the most powerful informal leaders are male.

Among any group, the person who has been cast in the role

of translator or sometimes assembly line lead tends to take on informal leadership responsibilities. This is well illustrated in a recent incident in which a Vietnamese translator was passed over for promotion in favor of another Vietnamese worker. This slight to his position was so offensive and his loss of face so grave that he resigned in order to minimize the humiliation. The strength of his leadership was seen when ten valued workers resigned with him as an indication of support. This case reminds us not to be surprised when workers refuse promotions in order to keep from being elevated above a countryman whom they regard as their social superior.

Should managers have difficulty ascertaining the identity of the informal leaders in their workplaces, you might advise them to observe the social dynamics of the workplace carefully. Have them watch for which individuals are getting preferential treatment, who is being addressed by a formal pronoun or title, and which workers are given the best seating in the lunch room or lounge. Try to find out who is asked for advice most often and which workers are given the most decision-making power. Finally, remember, just as it is all right to notice cultural differences, it is perfectly acceptable to acknowledge the existence of informal leadership and to ask immigrant workers who it is they particularly respect and look up to.

There are many practical reasons for managers to acknowledge and understand this hierarchy of leadership. Take, for example, the case of the corporation that had enough cultural awareness to give its largest Christmas bonus to the eldest member of its Asian work force, not to the person who had been on the job longest. This simple effort to communicate respect for the structure of the workers' culture went far toward improving relations and sustaining teamwork in the workplace. Allowing a newly arrived Cambodian worker to be accompanied on interviews by the informal leader, or using group leaders as conduits in your efforts to communicate information to your workers, are good ways to work effectively with these groups.

Informal leadership is clearly an essential element in many immigrant and ethnic cultures. These leaders are often powerful individuals who must be acknowledged and respected if we are to be successful in our efforts to communicate with and manage the culturally diverse work force.

Managers as Authority Figures. In this age of participative management, the notion of authority has taken on negative connotations. To be authoritarian conjures up images of dictatorships, discipline and tyranny. Valid as this perspective might be, managers need to be aware that many foreign-born workers are accustomed to looking up to authority figures and are therefore comfortable with a structured hierarchy of power in the workplace. Table 3–2 lists several ways in which this attitude affects the relationship between manager and worker. Let us examine each pair of statements in the table and look at how the difference between them can affect the manager's ability to sustain good working relationships:

Table 3–2
Attitudes toward Authority

Mainstream America	*Many Other Cultures*
1. Age is only one factor in determining who is in authority. A younger person can readily be placed over someone older.	Age is to be respected. If possible, a younger person should not be placed over someone who is older.
2. Gender has little to do with who will be in authority.	As a general rule, males are most likely to be found in positions of authority.
3. It is a good idea if the boss works alongside employees.	The boss should keep a formal distance from employees.
4. Employees should be encouraged to participate in decision making.	The boss who does not make his or her own decisions is weak.
5. Employees should feel comfortable questioning authority figures.	Employees should not question authority.
6. Workers are best motivated by persuasion.	Workers are best motivated by an authoritarian attitude.
7. Workers should be encouraged to act on their own.	Workers should not act without direct orders from the manager.
8. Workers have the right, even the obligation, to judge the performance of managers.	It is inappropriate for employees to judge the work of superiors.

Statement 1. We have already seen that age is still valued in many immigrant and ethnic cultures and that managers would be wise to find ways of communicating a similar respect for the elderly leaders of these groups. In the Soviet Union, young authority figures are clearly not as respected as their seniors. In Japan, age is often a prerequisite for a promotion, and in Mexico a younger employee is likely to defer to an older, more experienced worker.

This discrepancy in attitudes toward age can create difficulties when a younger manager is called upon to supervise older immigrant or ethnic employees. The danger is that the employee will have difficulty feeling respect and might even suffer loss of face by being supervised by someone younger.

We have seen one solution already. By giving the largest Christmas bonus to the eldest member of the group, respect can be shown and the danger of loss of face minimized. Another approach to the problem, which is remarkably easy to execute, is to address elder workers by their last names or, if appropriate to their culture, by the title Mr., Mrs., or Miss followed by a first name. This basic sign of respect is greatly appreciated by those who come from cultures in which this courtesy is routine.

Statement 2. Although there is still some progress to be made, the American corporation is growing increasingly receptive to the idea of placing women in authority positions. This is in contrast to the attitude found in many other countries where it is still unusual to find female managers. There are, however, notable exceptions; for example, women hold many prestigious posts in East India, Korea, and the Philippines.

Placing women in superior positions over immigrant men can sometimes create problems in eliciting the degree of respect necessary to do an adequate job. It must be added, though, that many foreign-born and ethnic workers realize that women enjoy more power in the United States. Because the workers know this, they are better able to adjust to and accept this new relationship.

Women supervisors and managers should find as many ways as possible to show personal respect for the male worker. The use of last names, the correct pronunciation of names, and making an effort to get to know the unique strengths and interests of each individual are ways in which to make the worker more comfortable and cooperative.

Statement 3. American managers feel that it is beneficial to productivity if they come down from their position of authority and roll up their sleeves to work beside employees. This has a positive effect on the native-born or assimilated worker who comes to perceive such a manager as a "regular" person. The reaction, however, from some immigrant workers can be quite different.

Asian workers in particular are inclined to interpret such behavior as both a sign of weakness and an indication that the manager feels that the worker is not doing an adequate job. This does not apply as much to Hispanic workers, who value the camaraderie with management but should be approached cautiously when the manager is a female and the Hispanic worker a male.

The solution is to compromise. It is not practical to ask American managers to ignore their instincts in this matter. The purpose of this book is not to ask managers to change their own culture but to find compromises that will bring harmony to the work setting. In this case, managers might explain to the Asian worker that their helping out does not reflect on the employee's performance but merely is a way of getting the job done faster. Another compromise is to maintain an otherwise fairly formal relationship with the Asian employee.

Statement 4. Current management practice in the United States strongly encourages the participation of workers in many decision-making processes. By contrast, in other cultures it is considered disrespectful of authority even to propose an idea. Indeed, in countries such as Greece, it is a weakness if the boss leaves decisions up to the employees. To go a step further, even questioning the decisions of the boss is considered a violation of the proper order of things. This is exemplified by the Thai proverb, "The leader has already been bathed in hot water," so, the sentence might continue, "knows how to do the job."

How can managers maintain the respect of immigrant workers while calling upon them to participate in their own management? How can they facilitate such participation when the worker has been taught that such behavior is inappropriate?

The answer is to maintain as much of a position of authority as possible: allow the worker to address you by your last name; maintain an appropriate, but not cold, social distance; make it clear that although you are calling on the worker for help, the final decisions are yours. This approach may be a bit unnatural for most American managers and is not, of course, appropriate in all cases. It is, however, a compromise in management style that can be very much worth the effort.

Statement 5. "Question authority" has come to be an edict that extends far beyond the turmoil of the 1960s. American workers are expected and encouraged to question the decisions of their managers, to debate with trainers in the training room, and to think for themselves. Elsewhere the situation is very different. For Asians, it begins in school where they are discouraged from questioning the wisdom of their teachers.

Managers who are accustomed to having workers voice their own ideas and speak up in meetings and in the training room are finding the apparent passivity of immigrant workers befuddling. There is a danger of managers' erroneously thinking that these workers have no ideas of their own or are uncommitted to their jobs. Another problem generated by this behavior is that the immigrant worker misses out on the chances for advancement that come with the voicing of new ideas.

You will notice, on the other hand, that some immigrant workers do not fall into this category at all. Swedes, for example, are accustomed to equal relationships with superiors and a healthy exchange of ideas.

The first step in the solution to this difficulty is to make certain that the workers know what you expect. Do not take it for granted that they know that you want them to question you, your managers, or your trainers. Second, utilize the informal group leaders. Tell them what you want and have them pass the request on to the other employees in a way that they will understand. You might also encourage the leader to demonstrate publicly what it is you are after. This is often the most immediate way of giving the workers permission to question authority. Finally, allow workers to express their ideas in writing and to do so anonymously. Although this approach has the disadvantage of your not knowing who the idea came from, it still is a way of allowing workers to voice their suggestions.

Statement 6. Few in corporate America would disagree with the position that persuasion is a more enlightened motivation strategy than coercion. But persuasion is by no means an approach with which the immigrant worker is familiar or even comfortable. Various studies have shown that Italian, French, Mexican, German, South American, Middle Eastern, and British workers tend to feel more comfortable with an authoritarian boss. In the Middle East, for example, it is unusual for a worker to say "no" to a boss for any reason. In Mexico and Asia, managers know not to carry this authoritarian attitude too far; to lose one's temper or swear is to lose the respect of one's workers.

Because of this difference, the soft approach of persuasion can sometimes be perceived of as a sign of weakness and indecisiveness. This perception, in turn, diminishes respect and can leave the worker feeling unsure of where responsibility lies.

Explaining to workers the expectations and behaviors of American management is an obvious but often neglected solution to difficulties such as this. It may seem almost too easy, but by simply telling the immigrant worker that motivation by persuasion is not a sign of weakness but is instead merely the American way of doing things, workers are quick to respond to this different concept of management.

Statement 7. In the United States, workers are encouraged to take the initiative on tasks; this is considered a sign of assertiveness, creativity, and skill. But other cultures take a different view of this behavior: to take independent action is to defy authority and to risk loss of face should the task be done incorrectly.

American corporations function well when independent initiative is the norm. Workers who wait for instructions at every turn tend to slow down productivity and create resentment among both coworkers and management.

The solution to this challenge was largely presented in the discussion of the fear of loss of face. It is a combination of informing the worker of what you expect—"In America we like it when workers act on their own"—and making a pact with the worker that, if he or she takes the initiative in an appropriate situation, you will verbally reward that step even if an error has been made. This, of course, is the hard part. What this amounts to is setting your priorities. In this case, it may be more important to encourage the taking of initiative than to be certain that every task is done correctly. The choice is up to each manager and depends on each individual situation.

Statement 8. If done with discretion, keeping an eye on the work of superiors is considered a virtue in American business. This applies not only to noting mistakes but to praising successes as well. In most other cultures, criticizing superiors is taboo. In many Asian cultures, it is even considered in poor taste to compliment a superior because such behavior has two implications: that the worker has a right to judge the manager and that the worker is somehow surprised at the achievement. In Japan, for example, a compliment to a boss might be stated as, "I hope that many people have the opportunity to read this report," a roundabout way of stating how valuable the report is.

On the surface, this reluctance to blame or praise managers may seem harmless, but when we look at it, the problem is similar to that caused by the worker who refuses to complain: management is unable to know where it stands in the eyes of its workers.

Anonymity is again helpful here. Since the main reason for this reluctance is the fear that such evaluation will appear disrespectful, inviting workers to submit critiques and compliments anonymously will encourage this behavior and is a compromise that can go far toward solving the problem.

It may be a mixed blessing that so many foreign-born and ethnic workers possess a great deal of respect for authority.

What matters is that managers make an effort to earn that respect, that they acknowledge its sincerity, and that they appreciate it for what it is.

Summary

Understanding the values of the foreign-born and ethnic worker is necessary if managers are to know how to interpret their behaviors, motivate change, and appreciate their needs. Remember these essential points:

- A reluctance to speak directly of negative things can arise from a desire to maintain harmony and balance in the relationship.
- Workers who do not take the initiative, praise themselves, or seek promotions may be afraid of defying authority, suffering embarrassment, or calling attention to themselves.
- Try to criticize foreign-born workers in private, to criticize the group as a whole if appropriate, to criticize an action rather than a person, and to reinforce desired behaviors.
- Get to know new applicants and employees.
- Communicate respect for the informal hierarchy of leadership characteristic of many ethnic and immigrant groups.
- Be careful not to draw excessive attention to the individual at the expense of the group.
- Share all your achievements with immigrant workers. You will be respected for it.
- Competition within groups is not always a productive approach. Cooperation and group goals are sometimes more culturally appropriate.
- Be sensitive to the fact that participative management and an informal relationship with the boss can make immigrant and ethnic workers uncomfortable.

4
Etiquette and Style
Respecting the Small Differences

> Do not necessarily do unto others as you would have them do unto you; after all, their tastes might be different.
> —Paraphrased from George Bernard Shaw

This chapter covers:

- The four functions of etiquette
- Techniques for compensating for differing rules of etiquette
- The culturally rooted desire for formality
- The importance of language etiquette
- Cultural variations in physical etiquette and body language
- Varying attitudes toward punctuality

The Little Things: Why They Matter

Pointing to someone with the index finger, hugging a person whom you have just met, and using crude language around superiors are violations of etiquette throughout the world. There are, however, other notions of proper behavior that are less universal. It is these variations in the rules of etiquette that can confuse and offend American managers on the one hand and their culturally diverse employees on the other.

The Vietnamese worker who does not hesitate to ask the price of a colleague's clothing, the Hispanic employee who refuses to call a manager by his or her first name, or the Japanese worker who is insulted by a compliment: each of these behaviors can create confusion and disharmony for the manager. At the same time, various immigrant and ethnic workers might be disoriented and offended when managers seem to rush the development of friendships, refuse to accept well-intended gifts, or beckon to them with upturned hands.

The purpose of this chapter is to clear up some of this confusion. Why is a whole chapter devoted to etiquette? After all, etiquette might be referred to as the poor relation of culture; it does not, for example, dictate our life choices like values do or, like language, allow us to communicate our loftiest thoughts. Why is there so much emphasis on such seemingly inconsequential things as touching and hand gestures? The answer is that these behaviors are not inconsequential. Every culture possesses rules of etiquette, and each of these rules serves a number of very important functions without which society would be far less harmonious and far more chaotic:

1. **Etiquette allows us to express the style of our culture.** By *style* is meant the values, atmosphere, and tone of a culture. The Asian desire for personal dignity and harmony is reflected, for example, in physical distance, gentle refusals, and limited eye contact. Similarly, the egalitarian American expresses his or her culture in the use of first names and casual dress. Etiquette symbolizes the larger values that make a culture unique.

2. **Etiquette lets us know what to expect in the behavior of others.** This works only when everyone is following the same rules—that is, when they have the same cultural background. Managers, for example, are likely to become confused when they discover that their immigrant workers do not wish to call the boss by his or her first name, a practice that would be pleasing and flattering to most mainstream Americans.

3. **Etiquette tells us how to make a good first impression on others.** In America we know, for example, what fork to

use at the dinner table and what sort of gift to bring the hostess. Again, however, everyone must be practicing the same etiquette for this system to work. A Middle Eastern male might expect a native-born manager to be pleased when he stands a foot away while conversing. To him this is an indication of real communication; the American manager may interpret this closeness as a sign of aggression. Because of differing rules of etiquette, the desired favorable first impression is not achieved.

4. **Etiquette allows us to feel confident in unfamiliar settings within our own culture.** When keeping an appointment with another professional, we know that we are expected to be on time or certainly no more than five minutes late. That is the etiquette of corporate America. Although we have not met the individual before, we have no doubt about how we are expected to behave. In cultures where time is more flexible, our punctuality might be perceived of as excessively fastidious, anxious, and even pushy.

Etiquette is powerful. Violations can easily offend and compliance can easily please. Before you become too apprehensive about what can happen if your managers commit a faux pas in the multicultural workplace, there is some reassurance.

First, it is the spirit of etiquette that matters, not the letter. What is most important is that managers grasp the general values and style of the immigrant's culture and that they have a basic respect for that style. If a professional violates the rules of formality that so many immigrants prefer by deliberately neglecting to use a colleague's title, it is likely that the colleague will be offended. But if that same manager genuinely appreciates the colleague's perspective and had neglected the title out of ignorance or even by accident, the immigrant may sense the innocence of the error and react accordingly.

Second, it is all right to ask the worker about etiquette differences. Acknowledging the reality of diversity and commenting on it is acceptable. In this case, to ask a worker about differences in etiquette is a practical approach. Often we neglect the simple solutions. By inquiring after a worker's needs and perspective, we not only learn how to avoid misunderstanding and conflict but also communicate an interest and respect that can only strengthen our working relationship.

Third, it is all right to observe the worker's actions. By watching the social behavior of culturally diverse employees, managers can quickly learn what is acceptable to them and what is not. If done in a way that does not make the worker self-conscious, this technique can provide the manager with much information about differences in etiquette and notions of proper behavior.

Fourth, it is all right to apologize. This is another obvious solution that tends to get lost in the complexity and anxiety of multicultural management. Perhaps it is pride, perhaps simply absentmindedness that makes managers forget that if a worker is inadvertently offended, a quick solution is to apologize. Due to the nature of many immigrant cultures, the worker is likely to deny that he or she felt offended—a denial designed to avoid any embarrassment to the manager. Nonetheless, the manager's apology will have been heard and the problem remedied.

Assessing the Manager's Reactions

Let us examine how we react to and feel about the behaviors and etiquette we encounter most often in the multicultural workplace. Like all of us, you probably find some of these culturally rooted behaviors charming, some bewildering, and some irritating. We need to be honest. Maybe we hate it when someone talks too much or are uncomfortable with what we see as excessive formality; possibly a limp handshake drives us crazy. No matter what your particular irritation, the important point is to identify it, learn more about it, and thereby gain the power to minimize your negative reaction.

Exercise 4–1 will help begin that process by asking you to identify your feelings about each behavior on the list. Circle the number that most closely reflects your emotional response. Once you become aware of what variations in etiquette are a problem for you, you will be better equipped to read the following pages

Exercise 4–1. Finding Your Etiquette Pet Peeves

Slowness in Building Relationships

Bothers Me   1   2   3   4   5   Bothers Me
a Little   a Lot

Extreme Formality

Bothers Me   1   2   3   4   5   Bothers Me
a Little   a Lot

People Who Speak Very Little

Bothers Me   1   2   3   4   5   Bothers Me
a Little   a Lot

People Who Talk a Great Deal

Bothers Me   1   2   3   4   5   Bothers Me
a Little   a Lot

People Who Speak Very Softly

Bothers Me   1   2   3   4   5   Bothers Me
a Little   a Lot

People Who Speak Loudly

Bothers Me   1   2   3   4   5   Bothers Me
a Little   a Lot

Vague Answers to Questions

Bothers Me   1   2   3   4   5   Bothers Me
a Little   a Lot

People Who Stand Very Close to Me

Bothers Me   1   2   3   4   5   Bothers Me
a Little   a Lot

Lack of Eye Contact

Bothers Me   1   2   3   4   5   Bothers Me
a Little   a Lot

Intense Eye Contact

Bothers Me   1   2   3   4   5   Bothers Me
a Little   a Lot

Limp Handshakes

Bothers Me   1   2   3   4   5   Bothers Me
a Little   a Lot

Relaxed View of Time/Deadlines

Bothers Me   1   2   3   4   5   Bothers Me
a Little   a Lot

with an eye toward learning as much about that particular behavior as possible. Watch for those issues that make you the most uncomfortable and disoriented.

The Social Graces: Remembering Our Manners

What is traditionally called good manners, formality, or, as grandmother would say, the social graces is regarded with varying degrees of favor in different parts of the United States. The general trend, however, is to think of any type of formal behavior as an indication of coldness, distance, and rigidity. This casual attitude—whether it is talking with our hands in our pockets, revealing intimate information about ourselves, or forgoing the use of professional titles—tends to make colleagues in other countries question the seriousness of our demands and culturally diverse workers in the United States feel confused about how much authority the American manager really has.

Although this attitude might be an unavoidable sign of the times, it can create problems for managers when working with foreign-born and ethnic employees who value formality and feel more comfortable when relationships are somewhat structured. The desire for formality varies, of course, among different groups. Koreans, for example, are slightly less formal than the Japanese, and Russians somewhat less than the French. But as a general guideline, it is safer to err in the direction of propriety than to assume that everyone prefers the American's informality.

Formality becomes particularly important when the worker is under emotional stress. For example, do not let courtesy slip away during an initial interview or when criticizing, coaching, or evaluating a worker. A good manager or human-resource professional will try to make employees feel more comfortable under circumstances such as these. The trick is not to project your own idea of comfort onto others. Whereas a casual, familiar attitude may suit the native-born applicant or worker, a formal approach will be more likely to put the immigrant employee at ease.

Good manners and formality can be expressed in many ways including how we move our bodies and how we carry on con-

versations. In addition, however, there are numerous other behaviors by which we demonstrate either a formal or informal
style. The following case study illustrates several of these. Pay
careful attention to items followed by a superscript letter.

> As manager of fifty plant workers at a small manufactur-
> ing firm in the Northeast, Mollie is constantly hiring new
> employees of different cultural backgrounds. Being very
> friendly and easygoing, she always greets the workers—
> many of them Korean and Puerto Rican—with great
> warmth and friendliness. Mollie has even been known to
> ask new workers to lunch on their first day to make
> them feel welcome.[a]
>
> At lunch, Mollie asks lots of questions as a way of
> getting to know each worker quickly. She inquires after
> their personal lives[b] and tries to set a casual tone by
> joking.[c] Mollie makes every effort to be egalitarian by
> using first names[d] and builds each worker's confidence by
> issuing compliments whenever possible.[e] She is careful to
> avoid alienating anyone, so she refuses to accept the gifts
> sometimes offered by the immigrant workers.[f] Above all
> else, she prides herself on treating everyone alike regard-
> less of his or her age or position in the community.[g]

On the surface, Mollie is a wonderful manager. The trouble is
that she is unaware that some cultures wish to be treated differently from others. Let us look at how the gaps in Mollie's
cultural awareness are reflected in the key points of the example.

a. *Managers should take their time developing relationships
with foreign-born and ethnic workers.* Native-born and assimilated Americans tend to form friendships quickly and base those
friendships on a fairly superficial knowledge of the other person.
We even go so far as to think of individuals who are slow to
open up as cold and reclusive. The situation is very different in
other cultures where the speedy formation of friendships is considered intrusive, unwise, and just plain bad manners. In this
case, Mollie's vigorous efforts to form good relationships may be
having the opposite effect.

Probably one reason that Mollie is making so many errors in cross-cultural etiquette is that she is not putting herself in the place of the worker; she is not trying to understand what he or she is experiencing when Mollie is so "friendly." One way for managers to avoid falling into this trap is for them to ask themselves how they would feel in a similar situation. How would you feel if a boss came up to you on your first day, put his or her arm around you, and began to gossip about company personnel? Almost certainly you would feel rushed, intruded upon, and decidedly uncomfortable—feelings identical to those experienced by the immigrant workers in our case study. Further, the possibility of sexual harassment aside, you are likely to lose some respect for the boss, who is, according to your cultural values, behaving inappropriately.

Forming relationships slowly may take some restraint on the part of American managers, but it will prove beneficial in the long run. Taking the time to get to know a worker can yield substantial dividends. Relationships that are formed slowly are deeper, last longer, and inspire more loyalty than those cultivated overnight. To the Asian, Hispanic, or Middle Eastern worker, the manager who rushes into camaraderie will probably be perceived of as superficial, untrustworthy, and even weak. Asians in particular interpret the premature revelation of information about oneself and the implied intimacy that goes with it as a sign of weakness and insincerity. Take it slow. The long-term benefits of doing so will be worth the restraint.

b. *Do not ask intrusive questions of workers.* Because ideas of what is intrusive vary from culture to culture, it is difficult to specify which questions are inappropriate in a particular situation. Asking a woman her age is almost universally offensive, but other topics will elicit varying responses. A fairly innocent inquiry about a worker's home life can appear rude to the native American, whereas a Hispanic employee would welcome any interest the manager shows in his or her family. Filipinos are inclined to ask fairly personal questions, which can be misinterpreted, even by the open American, as intrusive. In fact, such queries are designed to show warmth and respect.

Learn what is appropriate before asking questions that might make the foreign-born worker feel uncomfortable. To understand how such questions make the worker feel, it is helpful for the American-born manager to put himself or herself in the worker's position. When an intrusive question is asked of an immigrant worker, he or she feels the same sense of violation that American managers would experience if their boss asked something like, "How has your love life been lately?"

Note: If personal questions must be asked, explain to the worker why you need to obtain the information. This approach will relieve a lot of resentment by communicating to the worker that you are aware of, and respect, his or her differing point of view.

c. *Managers should avoid using jokes and sarcasm around workers of diverse cultures.* The problem here is not only that jokes tend to set an informal and intimate tone that can make workers uncomfortable but that humor generated out of American culture may not be understood by workers from other backgrounds. Although humor is a universal human trait, the specifics of what makes things funny vary from culture to culture. Because of this, jokes, and sarcasm in particular, might be taken literally or might offend someone who does not understand the joke.

Sarcasm is especially dangerous because it is a form of humor not found in every culture. To say playfully to a Middle Eastern worker, "You're a nut," or "You're crazy," is to risk compromising the relationship. In any case, sarcasm is a form of relating that smacks of intimacy and friendship—a tone that needs to be set cautiously.

Again, to put the manager in the worker's place, think what it would be like if a superior told an obscene joke in front of others; most managers would be offended and lose respect for that superior. This sort of behavior is particularly offensive to the Chinese worker who feels that humor is inappropriate between managers and employees.

d. *Managers should allow the use of last names and titles.* Attitudes toward the use of last names vary by region. In California it is commonplace for managers and even chief executive officers (CEOs) to be addressed by their first names. This informality is difficult for the more formal foreign-born and ethnic worker to accept. In Korea, only children, family, and one's closest friends are addressed by their first names. It is not unusual for workers to stop using the manager's name altogether rather than to address him or her in a manner they consider disrespectful and intimate.

Formality and manners is one way of defining relationships. Most immigrant workers are accustomed to regarding managers with respect. Thai workers are consistently formal with managers, even in a social setting. To call on any immigrant worker to use the more intimate first name is like asking American managers to summon their CEO by saying, "Hey, boss" or even "Hey, pal," a degree of informality alien to even the most casual southern Californian.

There is a compromise that sometimes works to relieve the tension between these two points of view. Asian and Middle Eastern workers, for example, are often comfortable calling the boss by the salutation "Mr.," "Miss," "Ms.," or "Mrs." and then the first name (Mr. Roy, Ms. Jenna, Mr. Paul, Mr. Charles), a usage that can work well and represents the kind of cultural compromise that contributes to a harmonious workplace. The reason that this is such a good solution is that, in many parts of Asia and the Middle East, respect is communicated in just this way: title and then the first name.

Note: When using the first or last names of your immigrant and ethnic workers, make certain that you pronounce them correctly. This important courtesy is an easy way of communicating respect for the individual and the culture.

e. *Be restrained with compliments.* This is not to say that sincere flattery is not considered good etiquette in most cultures but merely that managers should not automatically assume that everyone regards it as appropriate. Calling attention to the virtues of the individual is sometimes considered in poor taste, particularly by Asian workers. British workers, as well, would consider it better manners to state compliments in restrained terms and, if possible, in private.

If you do get overly zealous and issue elaborate flattery to the Asian worker, be aware that you are likely to be met with a denial, which is designed to maintain social harmony and should not be interpreted as evidence of low esteem. In addition, the Asian might respond with a laugh or giggle in an effort to cover up feelings of embarrassment. To issue a flowery compliment to an Asian is likely to make him or her feel the way an American manager would feel should he or she walk into a meeting, only to have the entire staff break into a standing ovation. Most would consider such behavior excessive and embarrassing.

Middle Eastern workers are inclined to feel very differently about the propriety of compliments. As a general rule, they are quick to flatter and pleased to be flattered. The key here is not to project your own cultural-specific ideas about what is proper and what is not. If you observe the behavior of diverse workers and are not afraid to ask questions, you will have a good idea of how to behave.

f. *Respect the small rituals of relationships.* Social rituals, whether in the home or in the workplace, form an important part of the culture of many ethnic groups. The exchange of food, for example, is a formality that carries with it meaning far beyond the satisfaction of hunger. Sharing food symbolizes, and cements, relationships. To refuse an offer of food because you are on a diet is to turn down far more than just the food itself; it is to reject the person doing the offering.

The same applies to the ritualistic proffering of gifts—a behavior that can lead to considerable misunderstanding in the American workplace. In America, the giving of gifts to the boss is usually interpreted as bribery. In other cultures, such offerings are proper social behavior and represent an expression of gratitude and deference, not a desire for special privilege.

The question of what to do in the face of such gifts is a complex one, which depends on the policy of the specific company and the value of the present. Generally, however, a refusal of a gift could be interpreted as an insult to the giver. This problem can be minimized by educating immigrant workers regarding management's policy toward gift giving. In the meantime, every effort should be made to avoid insult if the offering must be turned down.

g. *Respect the elderly.* Formality toward and respect for the elderly are gradually becoming less of a priority in American society. Although this change is also happening in other cultures, it is still largely accepted that the eldest of a group should be treated with deference and respect.

American managers should treat the elder members of an immigrant group with added formality, using last names and titles, escorting them to the door after visits to your office, and, if possible, standing up when they enter the room. This formality toward the oldest foreign-born workers will not cause them to lose respect for you as an authority figure. Quite the contrary, it will increase that respect. When respect is given to others, it very likely will be returned.

The Etiquette of Language   *Good*

The style of a culture is perhaps best illustrated in the use of language. We have all heard the adage, "It is not what you say that matters, but how you say it." In other words, your style of communication—the etiquette of the language you use—often dictates the success or failure of a conversation.

The way something is said can be more important than the actual content. The New Yorker who, in his or her excitement, interrupts a more sedate southern colleague is likely to offend the southerner, who may interpret that interruption not as enthusiasm but as rudeness. Even if the two parties agree on what is being discussed, the conversation is in danger of ending on a bad note. These kinds of misunderstandings can be avoided by taking the following steps:

1. Learn about cultural differences in the etiquette of language.

2. Make an effort, when appropriate, to match the communication style of the worker.

3. Avoid projecting your own cultural interpretations onto the behavior of others.

Language style consists of seven components: interruptions, silence and pauses, spontaneity, volume of speech, degree of directness, degree of embellishment, and ritualistic phrases.

Interruptions

Many cultures, especially those of the Far East, regard interruptions in conversation as extremely rude. This attitude is a manifestation of the formality common to many Asian countries. For the normally outspoken American, it is very difficult to resist the temptation to interrupt from time to time and speed the conversation along.

At the other end of the spectrum, French, Italian, and Arabic cultures are very comfortable with interruptions and with several people talking at once. This style of communicating is regarded as an expression of enthusiasm and commitment to the life of the conversation. When talking with someone who feels this way, you would be advised to recognize that such conversational gusto does not mean that the speaker is uninterested in what you are saying or that it is a sign of self-absorption.

It is situations like these that call into play rules 2 and 3. Match the communication style of the Asian worker by resisting the urge to interrupt, and avoid misinterpreting the talkative worker's behavior as a sign of rudeness or self-involvement.

Silence and Pauses

Mainstream Americans generally have fairly strong feelings about what pauses mean. As a way of promoting self-awareness, you might ask your managers to write down how they feel when a conversation is suddenly interrupted with a pause. Probable answers include, "It feels really awkward," "It usually means that someone is angry," or "I felt like such an idiot when I couldn't think of anything to say." Rarely will you get the kind of response that an Asian worker might give: "I felt so confident that there was no need to say anything," "I assumed the other party was silent because he was contemplating what I had just said," or "Sometimes it is just nice to take a moment to organize my thoughts." The Japanese proverb, "He who knows does not speak, and he who speaks does not know," summarizes the very different attitude Asian cultures have toward the etiquette of silence. A Japanese advertisement takes this sentiment even further: "Men keep silent and drink Sapporo beer."

You may have noticed that Asian workers tend to remain silent when in the presence of authority figures, a trait that can lead to the faulty impression that the worker is afraid or excessively shy. More likely such silences are designed to communicate respect for and deference to the superior.

Managers need to remember that silence is usually not an indication of something negative. Indeed, there is often a place for silence; it allows all parties an opportunity to collect their thoughts and formulate questions. Further, when criticizing or counseling an employee, pauses in the conversation allow time for the worker to translate what has been said and to contemplate its meaning.

As far as the behavior of the manager goes, too much talking and too few pauses can be experienced by the worker as meaningless jabber. Asians are inclined to interpret such behavior as a sign that little thought has gone into what you are saying, that you are lacking confidence, and that you are unfocused in your thinking. The solution here is to watch the behavior of your workers and to match that style when communicating with them—for example, by allowing pauses when speaking with Asians and avoiding them when dealing with Middle Easterners.

Spontaneity of Speech

Related to the issues of interruptions and silence is the spontaneity and rhythm with which particular groups speak. Asians, for instance, are inclined to speak only after careful deliberation. To blurt out a spontaneous idea in a brainstorming session would be considered both rude and unwise. Mainstream American culture, on the other hand, values spontaneity, as do the Italians, the French, and many of the Hispanic cultures. It is, in our eyes, a sign of creativity and enthusiasm. The problem with these differences lies in the meaning that is assigned to each speech pattern. The worker who is deliberate and careful in expression is in danger, for example, of being thought of as less intelligent and energetic than the more spontaneous and outspoken speaker.

Remember: just as an accent tells us nothing about the intelligence of a worker, the spontaneity and pace with which that same worker speaks has nothing to do with brightness or creativity, or even enthusiasm. It is instead a reflection of the individual's culturally dictated style of expression.

Volume of Speech

Nowhere are cultural differences in language etiquette more evident than in notions about how loudly a person should talk. In the United States, the basic position is that the individual should neither talk "too" loudly nor "too" softly.

The soft-spoken Asian who feels that to speak or laugh loudly is to be rude and disruptive can appear meek and retiring to the native-born manager. On the other hand, the southern European or Middle Easterner who tends to speak louder is often assumed to be aggressive, crass, and pushy. If managers are to function effectively in the multicultural workplace, they must avoid jumping to conclusions about personality based on how loud a person talks.

Rule 2 again becomes important here, especially with respect to conversations with soft-spoken workers such as the Hispanic female or Asian. Matching the volume of a worker's speech will lead to increased rapport. Experience shows that as the American speaks louder, the Asian progressively speaks softer, which causes the American to raise his or her voice still further. The difficulty is obvious, the solution simple: match the speaker's tone, and you have solved the problem.

Rule 3 is particularly important to remember when talking with someone who speaks loudly. Do not project your own culture's idea of what this behavior means; a loud tone of voice does not necessarily mean that the person is angry, upset, or demanding something.

Degree of Directness

Cultures possess differing notions about how direct one should be when stating negative facts. Asians, Hispanics, and East Indians tend to soften the negative. The Japanese might avoid saying "no" by answering an inquiry or request with another question. The Middle Eastern male is more direct and will speak emphatically.

This important part of language etiquette needs to be emphasized as a reminder to managers not to overreact to either approach. Do not assume that the Asian who avoids a confrontation is weak or dishonest or that the more direct Middle Easterner is aggressive or hostile. Most often, both cases are merely a matter of cultural style and have little to do with the speaker's feelings or intent.

Degree of Embellishment

Compared to other cultures, Americans are fond of plain speech. We greet people with a perfunctory "Hi," respond, Gary Cooper style, with a succinct "Nope," and when asked how we are, briefly say, "I'm fine" or "OK." Of course, this varies according to individual personality, but to be a person of few words is generally considered a virtue.

Native-born Americans tend also to avoid hyperbole. Although we are prone to speak of our highest building, tallest mountain, and highest-grossing company (and who can fail to notice the complete absence of "small" eggs in the grocery store), in everyday conversation we are very unlike the Italian, Middle Eastern, or Irish individual who takes pride in his or her ability to make flowery, embellished statements. Even the Japanese colleague, who tends to prefer understatement, may say, when coming across an overpriced object, "I am overpowered with admiration," rather than simply stating that it is "too expensive." Middle Easterners in particular, value language and what it can do. They are likely to repeat statements and embellish them to the point that native-born Americans are inclined to question their credibility.

Managers need to be careful not to overreact to the elaborate statements that some cultures prefer. They are usually not intended as dishonesty and merely reflect what is considered to be a gracious and even artistic form of expression.

Ritualistic Phrases

The English language is filled with phrases designed to fulfill routine social functions. Statements such as "I'll see you later," "Let's get together sometime," or "I'll talk to you again soon" are often intended merely as social amenities and are not expected to be taken seriously. This is carried to an extreme when we greet someone with "How are you?" and are surprised and dismayed when he or she actually answers us in detail. In America, the question is no more than a form of greeting. To the Dutch, on the other hand, our refusal to stop and listen is perceived of as rude and self-centered.

The problem in the multicultural workplace is that the worker who has been raised in another culture might be unaware of the ritualistic purpose of such phrases. Cases have been reported in which employees were told, "Come to dinner sometime," only to have the worker show up without a more specific invitation. This error illustrates not only an unfamiliarity with the ritualistic purpose of many American invitations but also an understandable ignorance of American social norms. This is not to say that managers need to curtail their use of such phrases but merely that they should be aware that some workers might, out of ignorance of American etiquette, take them literally.

Physical Etiquette

Let us move on to the physical expression of culturally specific ideas about the proper way to behave. The material contained in this section might also be called "nonverbal language" or "body language." It could be argued that this information should have been covered in the discussion of how to overcome language barriers. It has been included here, however, because the focus of this discussion is less on how these behaviors function to communicate and more on how they reflect the cultural value of etiquette and, in most cases, formality. Before entering into the body of our discussion, it might be helpful for you and your managers to take the quiz in exercise 4–2 to see how aware you are of cultural differences in nonverbal language. The correct answers to the questions are found in the following discussion.

The Significance of Space

Someone once said, "Whoever controls the space, controls the situation." The space we maintain around our bodies—also referred to as proxemics—reflects a desire to control who gets close to us and under what circumstances. Ideas about how close is close vary from culture to culture and reflect the style and tone of the society at large. The following list summarizes some of these variations:

0–18 inches: Middle Eastern males, eastern and southern Mediterraneans, and some Hispanic cultures.

18 inches–3 feet: Mainstream Americans and Western Europeans.

3 feet or more: Asians (Japanese the farthest) and many African cultures.

American ideas of proper distance fall somewhere in the middle of those held by most cultures. The spread between 18 inches and 3 feet takes into consideration the nature of the relationship with the other person. The correct answer, for example, to question 1 in exercise 4–2 is that Americans, on average, stand 2 feet away when conducting business.

Few other areas of etiquette are more important and, fortunately, easier to respect than ideas of how much space should be

Exercise 4–2. Body Language: A Cross-Cultural Quiz

1. Mainstream American culture dictates that in business relationships, we keep a distance of:

   a. 18 inches
   b. 2 feet
   c. 3 feet

2. It is inappropriate to touch Asians:

   a. on the arm
   b. on the head
   c. on the hand

3. *True or false*: Mainstream Americans tend to maintain eye
   contact for only 1 second at a time.

4. *True or false*: A smile is one of the few forms of nonverbal
   language that has the same meaning throughout the world.

5. The groups that tend to have the firmest handshakes are:

   a. Vietnamese and Filipinos
   b. British and French
   c. Germans and Americans

6. *True or false*: Americans are unique in their feeling that pointing at another person is rude.

7. Beckoning with upturned fingers, palm facing us, as we do in
   America, is offensive to which of the following peoples:

   a. Mexicans
   b. Filipinos
   c. Vietnamese
   d. All of the above

8. Gesturing with the left hand is considered in poor taste for
   those immigrants who are:

   a. Hindus
   b. Muslims
   c. Buddhists

kept between parties in a conversation. There are some circumstances under which notions of proxemics are particularly important. These are the occasions when workers are in danger of feeling emotionally or even physically threatened if their body space is invaded—for example, when a worker is undergoing the stress of a job interview or, worse, is meeting with the manager or human-resource professional for a performance review.

Still more delicate are those times when the manager must discipline or criticize a worker. Under those circumstances, it is especially important not to stand too close and to avoid standing over the worker, stances that can make the worker feel threatened and defensive. Employees who feel defensive have difficulty hearing, much less agreeing with, what the manager is saying. The fact is that the choices we make regarding bodily space can have a powerful impact on the success of our interpersonal relationships.

The Meaning of a Touch

The verb *to touch* comes from the Latin *touchare* ("to strike lightly"). It would be wise for managers to keep this etiology in mind when considering whether to touch the foreign-born and ethnic worker. Although some cultures are more liberal in their attitudes toward touching than others, even the most tactile groups have strict rules of propriety and etiquette. To touch at the wrong time can represent a violation of cultural etiquette and can also risk misunderstandings.

Not surprisingly, the general guidelines for proxemics already discussed also apply to the issue of touch. Asians tend to resist being touched, especially on the back, head, and shoulder. The answer to question 2 in exercise 4–2 is that Asians prefer not to be touched on the head; this applies particularly to small children. Managers need to resist the urge to tousle the hair of an Asian child. It is also inappropriate to put one's arm on the back of a chair in which an Asian worker is sitting. On the other hand, to toss an object to a Filipino rather than hand it directly can be offensive in that it implies you might have some reluctance about touching him or her.

Note: You may notice that Filipino females are very warm and tactile toward each other; holding hands while walking, for example, is not unusual. Do not let this display of comradeship confuse the issue; such signs of affection are carefully confined to particular relationships and do not indicate a general receptivity to indiscriminate touching.

The British and Israelis have similar restrictions about touching. Managers who have difficulty understanding the importance of restraint might try imagining how they would feel if a stranger spontaneously put his or her arms around them; the sense of intrusion and impropriety is the same as that felt by immigrant workers.

Notions of appropriate touching are mixed in Hispanic and Middle Eastern cultures. Generally these groups are comfortable with physical closeness; Mexican males, for example, are likely to stand close to a male colleague while speaking and to hold him by the lapel, shoulder, or forearm. Similar behavior is found among Middle Eastern men, although if they are Muslims care would be taken not to touch with the left, or "toilet," hand.

The situation changes, however, when the parties are of different sexes. Touching across gender lines should be strictly avoided in professional situations. A female manager who even casually puts her arm around the shoulder of the immigrant male worker is risking a loss of respect. Since so much is at risk if an error is made, the cardinal rule must be to avoid touching unless it is obviously appropriate. I am not suggesting that managers need to appear cold and aloof but merely that they should find alternative ways of communicating warmth.

The Meaning of Eye Contact

The answer to question 3 in exercise 4–2 is true. In American culture it is considered appropriate to maintain eye contact for about 1 second and then to look away. To do otherwise is to appear threatening; if we do not maintain any eye contact at all, we may seem uninterested, shy, or dishonest.

Maintaining eye contact for 1 second represents a middle range when compared to the rest of the world. Middle Eastern,

Hispanic, southern European, and French cultures generally advocate very direct eye contact. For other groups—Asians, native Americans, East Indians—it is far more appropriate to look away. For Cambodians, it is even considered flirtatious for a person to look at someone of the opposite sex in the eye.

To make things still more complicated, there is more to cultural variations in eye contact than just the length of time the gaze is held. One of these complexities has to do with the roles the two parties are playing in the conversation. There are, for example, differing ideas about the etiquette of eye contact between Anglo-Americans and some African-Americans. Anglo-Americans consider it proper to maintain eye contact when the other party is speaking but to allow the eyes to wander somewhat when they themselves are talking. For African-Americans, the situation is just the opposite: eye contact is maintained while the African-American is talking and allowed to wander when the other person begins to speak. Unfortunately, this difference can lead the Anglo person to feel, mistakenly, that the African-American is aggressive and involved when he or she is speaking but ultimately is uninterested in what the other party has to say.

By learning about and understanding such cultural differences, managers can easily avoid this sort of misunderstanding. Table 4–1 lists some other areas of confusion that might arise.

Managers confronted with a worker whose idea of proper eye contact is not shared by mainstream American culture should do nothing. As long as the manager does not misinterpret the behavior (as hostility or dishonesty, for example), it makes no difference how long the worker does or does not look you in the eye.

This is an area of etiquette where it is not appropriate to match the behavior of the worker. To look away deliberately or maintain unnaturally direct eye contact will only make the manager uncomfortable and can create unnecessary tension in the relationship.

The Face and Smile

Is the smile a universal way of communicating goodwill and cheerfulness? Probably. However, ideas about the fine points of

Table 4–1
Variations in Eye Contact

Very direct eye contact
  Groups: Middle Easterners, some Hispanic groups, the French
  Misinterpretation: Hostility, aggressiveness, intrusiveness, bossiness
  Correct interpretation: A desire to express an interest, a desire to communicate effectively

Moderate eye contact
  Groups: Mainstream Americans, northern Europeans, the British
  Misinterpretation: Lack of interest in what is being said
  Correct Interpretation: A desire not to appear aggressive or intrusive

Minimal eye contact
  Groups: East Asians, Southeast Asians, East Indians, native Americans
  Misinterpretation: Lack of interest, lack of intelligence, dishonesty, lack of understanding, fear, shyness
  Correct interpretation: A desire to show respect, a desire to avoid intrusion

when to smile do vary from culture to culture. The answer to question 4 is false; a smile does not have the same meaning in all situations throughout the world. Mainstream Americans, for example, generally employ a smile freely. To them it represents goodwill and is a safe way of communicating friendliness and optimism. To many Soviet immigrants, on the other hand, a smile, especially if proffered by authority figures, can signal a frivolity and lightness that is inappropriate to the situation. For Middle Easterners a smile might be used to placate a colleague and avoid conflict. In France, to smile at someone on the street is considered an inappropriate intrusion or invitation. For many Asians, a smile often covers up discomfort, embarrassment, or anger. We have seen, for example, that the Asian who does not understand what is being said might smile or laugh as a means of diffusing and concealing the embarrassment of the moment. The Korean proverb, "The man who smiles a lot is not a real man," clearly illustrates the attitude Korean culture holds concerning the significance of a smile.

This is not to say that American-born managers should minimize their own culturally conditioned reliance on a smile. It merely means that we need to become aware that a smile does not carry a universal meaning.

Handshakes

One of the important functions of etiquette is to allow us to make a favorable first impression. The nature of a person's handshake is certainly one of the main ways in which an impression is made; the brusk handshake of the German leaves us with an assumption of sternness, and the gentle grasp of most Asians tends to make us feel that he or she is weak or indecisive.

These impressions are likely to be incorrect. What we are experiencing on these occasions is not a reflection of a personality or a character but merely an instance of what is considered a proper handshake by that individual's culture. Table 4–2 gives an idea of how various cultures differ in their idea of a proper handshake. As you can see, the answer to question 5 is *c*: Germans and Americans have the firmest handshake.

Managers should be sure not to project their own idea of a good handshake onto others. The character or personality of the worker whose handshake is either firmer or gentler than the American norm should not be judged by the nature of his or her grasp.

Handshakes provide a good opportunity for the manager to match the cultural style of a worker. Relax your usually firm

Table 4–2
Handshakes

Americans: Firm

Germans: Brusk, firm, repeated upon arrival and departure

French: Light, quick, not offered to superiors, repeated upon arrival and departure

British: Soft

Hispanics: Moderate grasp, repeated frequently

Middle Easterners: Gentle, repeated frequently

Asians: Gentle; for some, shaking hands is unfamiliar and uncomfortable (an exception to this is the Korean who generally has a firm handshake)

grip when shaking the hand of an Asian, for example, or adapt to the tighter grasp of the German. These adjustments can make both parties more comfortable and can guarantee a good first impression.

Hand Gestures

Second only to touch, it is in the movement of the hands that we are most likely to bring offense to workers from other cultures. It is also in this area that professionals tend to be the most self-conscious. It is not unusual to hear a manager say, "I sometimes feel that I have to sit on my hands to avoid offending someone." This section is designed to help managers overcome some of this fear by learning those gestures that are most often found in the multicultural workplace and that are most likely to be offensive.

Pointing. Pointing is considered not so much as offensive but certainly as poor etiquette in American culture. The answer to question 6 in exercise 4–2 is false. This attitude is almost universal. In Asian cultures, proscriptions against pointing are very strong. To point at an Asian worker with the index finger is considered both offensive and intrusive. Some Asian groups even consider it poor taste to point at an object.

The etiquette of pointing goes beyond the question of who or what to point at and includes rules about how to point. In Thailand, China, and much of the rest of Asia, any necessary pointing is generally done with the entire hand. In Hong Kong, one points with the middle finger, and in Malaysia, it is proper to point with the thumb.

Managers would be wise to avoid pointing altogether. Why take a chance of offending someone when this simple restraint can easily solve the problem?

Beckoning. Mainstream Americans beckon to others with up-turned fingers, palm facing the body—a gesture that is deeply offensive to Mexicans, Filipinos, and Vietnamese. The answer to question 7 in exercise 4–2 is *d:* all of the above. In the Philippines, for example, this is the way to beckon to animals, underlings, and prostitutes. To understand how offensive this gesture can be, remember what it feels like to be called with a crooked index finger; it can be very humiliating and infuriating. A more appropriate way to beckon is with the palm facing toward the ground and the fingers moving, a gesture similar to the way Americans wave goodbye.

Signs of Approval. Ironically, our gestures of validation—the "OK" sign, the "thumbs-up" signal, and the "V" for victory (especially if done with the palm facing the face; even Winston Churchill used to make this mistake) are among the most offensive to other cultures. All three have strong sexual connotations, as does our "thumbing-a-ride" gesture. For immigrants as diverse as Soviets and Hispanics and dozens in between, to use any of these gestures is to risk bringing serious offense.

Although most immigrant and ethnic workers realize that managers probably do not mean to be offensive when using these signals, there still is likely to be a culturally rooted conditioned association with the gesture that can make the worker feel embarrassed or uncomfortable. Managers can avoid any difficulty by eliminating these gestures from their vocabulary of body language.

Signaling "No". There are a lot of reasons why it is sometimes hard to know if someone from another culture is telling us "yes" or "no." Here is a case in which hand gestures can save the day. In Mexico and the Middle East, a "no" is indicated by a back-and-forth movement of the index finger. This unmistakable signal can clear up at least one of our cross-cultural communication challenges.

The Left Hand. Gesturing or handing something with the left hand is offensive to many Muslim workers, who regard this hand as the "toilet hand." The answer to question 8 in exercise 4–2 is obviously *b:* Muslims. It is not that managers need to become excessively self-conscious about the use of this hand but merely that it is something to bear in mind when working with Muslim employees and colleagues.

Note: Placing the index finger to the lips and making a "shh" sound to signal silence is also considered obscene by many Middle Eastern workers.

Managers are prone to feeling especially self-conscious about the danger of making an offensive gesture. Although there is some reason for this fear, we can all take comfort from the fact that if an inappropriate hand signal is genuinely accidental or is made out of ignorance of cultural differences, it is likely that the immigrant and ethnic worker will realize this and not take offense at the gesture.

The Legs and Feet

American culture does not have a lot to say about the proper positioning of the legs. About all that is mentioned is that at a business meeting, it is inappropriate, particularly for women, to sprawl in a chair with knees open. In a way this is surprising because other cultures have fairly stringent rules of "leg etiquette."

Crossing the legs, for example, is in poor taste among most Asians and Middle Easterners. One of the reasons for this restriction is that when the legs are crossed, the bottom of the foot is showing and the toe is pointing at someone—both of which are considered rude and offensive. A Soviet variation on this restriction is that is it rude to place the ankle on the knee. These are rules that managers do not necessarily need to match. It is enough to be aware that some immigrant workers will follow them.

Punctuality: The "Politeness of Princes"?

According to northern European culture, "Punctuality is the politeness of princes." Originating somewhere in the eighteenth century and coming to full acceptance during the industrial revolution, punctuality has come to be associated with productivity, reliability, and even intelligence.

Nowhere else, except perhaps in Germany, has this edict been more accepted than in corporate America. Time is precious to most Americans; it is a commodity to be "used," "saved," "spent," "wasted," "lost," and even "killed."

Although the specifics vary in different regions of the nation, it is generally thought that to be late to work, late for an appointment, or late with a deadline is to be lazy, sloppy, and, certainly rude. In many parts of the country, 5 minutes is considered a significant unit of time—that is, the point after which it is acceptable to feel offended at having been kept waiting or anxious at having been delayed. The French are slightly more relaxed, with 15 minutes perceived of as a significant delay.

The challenge for managers in this regard is that most of the rest of the world has a much more casual attitude toward precise timekeeping. In much of the Middle East, to keep someone waiting for an appointment is in no way considered a sign of lack of interest or rudeness; the clock is simply not important. The Saudi proverb, "Haste comes from the devil," sums this difference up, as does the linguistic oddity that in the English language clocks are said to "run," in Spanish to "walk," and in native American dialects simply to "tick."

The cultures that tend to be the most relaxed about time are the Hispanic cultures, the Caribbean groups, the Middle Eastern cultures, and the Filipinos—the last as a result of three hundred years of Spanish occupation. Northern Europeans and Asians generally value punctuality. The most likely exception to this is the Korean, whose penchant for being on time varies according to the situation and relationship.

The inclusion of this topic here does not imply that it is all right for workers to be chronically late for work, appointments, meetings, or deadlines. However, in order to motivate behavior change, managers need to understand why a worker is behaving in a particular way. By recognizing that chronic lateness might be based not in laziness, lack of commitment, or stupidity but in culturally rooted misunderstandings about the expectations of American management, managers can design effective strategies for remedying the situation.

Summary

Although he lived and wrote in turn-of-the-century Ireland, George Bernard Shaw seemed to have a good grasp of the complexities of cultural differences when he modified the Golden Rule to read, "Do not do unto others as you would they should do unto you. Their tastes may not be the same." Just because we are equal does not mean we are the same. One of the greatest areas of diversity lies in what might seem like the inconsequential area of etiquette—the small rules that can have a big impact on relationships.

Even in the absence of specific knowledge about every cultural variation in etiquette, the following general rules will help diminish the chance of conflicts and misunderstandings:

- Etiquette makes a difference.
- The spirit of the rules is more important than the letter.
- Ask your workers for details about their etiquette.
- Observe your employees' behaviors.
- Apologize if you make an error.
- Become aware of what bothers you.
- Proceed slowly.
- Err in the direction of formality.
- Match etiquette behaviors when appropriate.
- Do not overreact to varying cultural styles.
- Avoid projecting your own culture onto others.

5
Motivation Strategies
Achieving Employee Behavior Change

You must either know his nature and fashions and so lead him . . .
or his ends and so persuade him.

—Francis Bacon

This chapter covers:

- Techniques for overcoming resistance to behavior change
- Information on how to interpret behavior correctly
- Methods for explaining what you expect from your workers
- Guidelines for compromising with the immigrant and ethnic worker
- The value of speaking the worker's cultural language
- Insights into culturally specific felt needs
- Guidelines on how to reinforce desired behaviors

In the sixteenth century, Francis Bacon summed up the essentials of motivation when he said of those whom we wish to persuade, "You must either know his nature and fashions and so lead him . . . or his ends and so persuade him." Under the best of circumstances, understanding a worker's "nature" and "ends" in order to design effective motivation strategies is not easy.

Individuals are diverse. One worker might value and strive for more money, whereas another is much more responsive to the prospect of increased authority, time off, or something as simple as a better parking spot.

Cultural diversity in the workplace makes the development of effective motivation strategies even more complex. As we shall see, something that motivates a worker from one ethnic or immigrant group might be meaningless to another. As Bacon realized, motivation is nothing more than an effort to assess the individual's needs and to match those needs to the company and its goals. This chapter will help you make the kind of matches that promote teamwork and improve productivity.

There are six steps to cross-cultural motivation:

1. Interpret the behavior correctly.

2. Explain your expectations and the expectations of American management.

3. Compromise.

4. Speak the worker's cultural language.

5. Honor felt needs.

6. Positively reinforce the desired behavior.

Each of these steps can be used as part of an overall strategy or taken individually depending on the specifics of the situation.

Throughout the previous chapters, we have looked at a number of core behaviors commonly found in the multicultural workplace. Among these are:

- Hesitance to take independent initiative on tasks
- Reluctance to complain or make negative statements
- Failure to admit lack of understanding
- Reluctance to seek or accept promotions
- Reluctance to praise self
- Speaking of foreign languages in the workplace

These behaviors will be used to illustrate the six steps. Of course, each technique can be applied to any behavior—not just those discussed here. You will find that these approaches are particularly effective for behaviors that are most deeply rooted in differing values and expectations.

Overcome Resistance to Change

Any thinking human being will resist being changed by someone else. Such resistance can be especially strong among foreign-born and ethnic workers. Before managers can effectively use any motivation techniques, they must understand the reasons for this resistance and learn how to overcome it.

Much reluctance to change arises from the worker's mistaken impression that the manager is trying to change his or her basic values and culture. Although you are concerned only with modifying one specific bit of behavior, workers might assume that you are interested in nullifying their entire culture.

Understandably, and rightly, many immigrants are committed to maintaining their cultural identity. When this identity is threatened—whether the threat is real or imagined—the worker naturally feels considerable anxiety. For most of us, our culture is a part of our sense of self, our essential identity. When our culture is compromised, so too are we.

Behavioral scientists know that in order for change to take place, the subject—in this case, the culturally diverse worker—must feel psychologically safe and secure enough to make that adjustment. Anxiety about losing one's cultural identity, one's way of life, can only interfere with any receptivity to new ideas and behaviors. A defensive reaction is even more likely to set in when the employee is already in a state of culture shock—disoriented and threatened by being immersed in a strange culture.

Exercise 5–1 will help you and your managers better understand these feelings of fear and defensiveness. Each question assumes that you have been suddenly transported to a different culture and are being asked to do something that does not fit with your culture's most basic principles.

Exercise 5–1. Understanding Cultural Threats

1. If a manager told me that I was never to take the initiative on tasks but wait to be told to make every move, I would feel . . .

2. If someone tried to convince me that I should keep everything that goes wrong from the manager and never complain, I would feel . . .

3. If my supervisor told me that I should always pretend to understand what has been said and never ask any questions, I would feel . . .

4. If a manager told me to stay in my place and never seek promotions, I would feel . . .

5. If someone told me that I was never to say anything about my accomplishments or skills, I would feel . . .

To the first question, you probably responded with such feelings as "diminished," "trapped," "insulted," and "dominated." Similarly, you might have felt, in response to question 2, that the manager was not accepting his or her responsibility, that you were being asked to be dishonest, and, certainly, that the manager was not very good at his or her job.

If told to pretend to understand everything that is said, most of us would feel as if we were being asked to be dishonest. We also might conclude that the manager does not care whether we learn the material.

Being forbidden to strive for promotions would call up instant feelings of bondage, frustration, and insult. Similarly, if we are not allowed to speak of our achievements in appropriate settings, we tend to feel that they do not matter, that we might as well not strive anymore, and that we are less accomplished than we previously thought.

The specifics of your responses are not the important point here. The point is that when you are asked to behave in ways that counter the values of your upbringing—in the case of this exercise, straightforwardness, ambition, and pride—your emotional reactions can be very strong. Among those emotions are likely to be confusion, resentment, possibly anger, and certainly resistance.

A second reason for resistance to behavior change is the worker's belief that the manager, in requesting a different way of doing things, is implying that the worker's old method was deficient and wrong. (We will see in a moment how to overcome this problem.)

Finally, foreign-born and ethnic workers might be reluctant to adapt new behaviors because the behaviors seem very strange to them. To ask an Asian to praise himself or herself in front of a group, for example, is like asking the native-born manager to walk into a party and immediately begin bragging to the first stranger who comes along. For Hispanics to seek promotions over countrymen older than themselves would be like asking the American-born manager to sabotage the professional progress of a dear friend just to advance within the company.

As far as taking the initiative on tasks, it would be like expecting a native-born worker to stride into the boss's office and begin cleaning his or her desk without having been asked to do so. To expect an Asian worker to complain about something is like expecting yourself to keep the boss informed of every tiny negative event that happens on the job. None of these actions feels right.

This should give you and your managers some idea of what the culturally different worker feels when asked to meet the expectations of American managers. These are, of course, generalities that do not apply to every immigrant or ethnic worker, but they do help make the point.

Now that we understand the roots of resistance, it is time to look at how this defensiveness can be overcome. Each of the following six steps to cross-cultural motivation is designed in some way to diminish resistance. There are, however, two other techniques that must be mentioned: the use of reassurance and the bestowing of power.

The truth is, or ought to be, that managers are concerned only with maintaining a properly functioning workplace, not with altering any personally held beliefs or cultural values. By reassuring the worker that you are merely asking him or her to change an isolated behavior, that you have no interest in modifying his or her entire culture, a great deal of resistance can be overcome. Reassurance should also be provided that, by asking the worker to behave differently, you are not implying that his or her previous way of acting was wrong or deficient but merely that it did not function well in the American workplace.

A second way to overcome resistance is to give the worker as much power as possible. People do not resist changing; they resist being changed. By including employees in the decision to change, they are more likely to make the behavior their own and to stick to it with greater commitment.

Do not just tell workers what to do; ask them how far they are prepared to go in modifying their usual way of acting. By giving them the power to participate in the decision and in the specific details of the change, you will decrease anxiety and defensiveness and increase the chance of compliance. Even if you find that your workers do not wish to contribute to this decision because of discomfort with participative management, you will still have asked for their comments, a gesture that is itself empowering.

⎰ ⎱ Interpret the Behavior Correctly

The first of the six steps to successful cross-cultural motivation is to understand why a worker is behaving in a particular way. This step is important for two reasons. First, it communicates to workers that you respect them enough to learn what might be very culturally specific reasons for particular attitudes and behaviors. You thus avoid the trap of projecting your own cultural explanations onto the behaviors of others. When you show this respect and interest, you will make the worker feel less defensive and be far more willing to cooperate.

The second reason for correctly interpreting behavior has to do with the development of appropriate and successful motivation strategies. Only if we understand why a person behaves in a particular way can we design the correct approach to modify that behavior. Assessing why workers do what they do can be difficult enough when you all share the same background; it is even more likely to result in errors when a given worker's values and expectations of proper employee behavior are different from your own.

The following case study addresses the issue of speaking a foreign language in the workplace. Although the legal and practical consequences of this practice vary substantially among industries—it is more problematic, for example, in hospitals than in manufacturing plants—it is an issue of importance to many employers. Clearly there are times when the speaking of other languages, especially around colleagues, clients, and customers, can be disruptive to teamwork and to the efficient operation of the workplace.

> Shea is a supervising nurse on the night shift of a large metropolitan hospital. Her staff consists of many nurses who were born and trained overseas. One of her nurses, Cecilia, is from the Philippines and is a wonderful caregiver except that she repeatedly is discovered speaking Tagalog within earshot of her patients. Shea assumes that Cecilia is doing this so that she can gossip with her friends and talk about the patients without being understood.

Although they like Cecilia, some of her patients have begun to complain, and it is obvious that they have lost faith in Cecilia's ability to provide effective care. Shea finally got fed up with the situation and became angry with Cecilia in front of the other nurses. Because Shea knew that Cecilia has a great deal of respect for authority, she was surprised to find that Cecilia has continued to speak her own language around the patients.

What might Shea have done wrong? Why didn't Cecilia respond to her supervisor's obvious dissatisfaction? The answer is that Shea failed to understand the true meaning of Cecilia's behavior. If Shea had more knowledge of immigrant workers and had tried to put herself in Cecilia's place, she might have been able to resolve the problem more successfully.

Shea would have realized that Cecilia was probably not speaking Tagalog in order to gossip behind the backs of colleagues and patients. Instead, she more likely was using her own language in an effort to function more efficiently in the often stressful health care setting. Possibly she did not realize what she was doing and simply slipped into her language when she was rushed or fatigued. She might also have been lonely and felt the need to communicate with someone who would readily understand her.

If Shea understood these possible motivations—had interpreted Cecilia's behavior correctly—she would have been in a better position to design an effective strategy. Perhaps Cecilia needed a refresher course in the English vocabulary most often used in her job, some ideas of how to relieve the stress that caused her to forget, and maybe a reminder regarding her right to communicate with her Tagalog-speaking friends on breaks or when away from the patients.

Throughout the last few chapters, a lot of discussion has been directed toward the proper interpretations of various behaviors. Because of the importance of this material, Table 5–1 has been compiled to serve as a quick review.

Each of these behaviors has been discussed elsewhere in the book. The point here is that if we fail to understand the reasons

Table 5-1
Correct Interpretations

Behavior	Interpretation
Hesitance to take independent initative on tasks	Respect for authority, fear of loss of face, desire for anonymity, fear of job loss
Reluctance to complain or make negative statements	Desire for harmony in relationships, respect for authority, compassion for manager, fear of negative reflection on group, fear of job loss
Failure to admit lack of understanding	Fear of loss of face, fear of embarrassment for manager, fear of not understanding the material if it is repeated
Reluctance to seek or accept promotions	Desire for anonymity, belief in leaving things to fate, desire not to be elevated above the group, respect for informal group hierarchy, desire to fulfill one's present role, fear of loss of face, varying personal needs, wishes of family members
Reluctance to praise self	Desire for anonymity, desire not to be set apart from the group
Speaking of foreign languages in the workplace	Fatigue, loneliness, forgetfulness, unconscious response to stress and crises, desire for efficiency

for a behavior, it is nearly impossible to know how best to motivate the desired change.

Explain Your Expectations

This may seem like an obvious step; nevertheless, often managers fail to explain what they want and why they want it. Immigrant workers are rarely formally instructed in the values of U.S. culture and even less often in the desires of American management. They are never told, for example, that it is appropriate and expected to call in if they are going to be late, to take the initiative on tasks, seek promotions, or keep the manager informed of problems in the workplace.

Explaining what we want from others is not easy. Often it is

Exercise 5–2. Explaining Your Expectations
to Employees

1. Taking the initiative on tasks

2. Voicing complaints and saying negative things

3. Admitting lack of understanding

4. Seeking and accepting promotions

5. Praising oneself

6. Speaking English in the workplace

---

the most familiar procedures, policies, and expectations that are the most difficult to articulate. Exercise 5–2 is designed to give you and your managers an opportunity to practice the task of figuring out what you really want and then explaining those desires to employees. In a few sentences, write what you expect from workers with respect to each of the behaviors listed in the exercise.

Probably you and your managers will discover that it is not so easy to explain clearly that which is so obvious to you. Let us move through each of these and see what might be said to the worker.

1. *Taking the initiative on tasks:* "In the United States, taking the initiative reflects well on workers. To do so helps the manager and enables the workplace to run more efficiently. Also, native-born managers feel that it is good to take chances—'Nothing ventured, nothing gained,' 'We learn from our mistakes.' If you take the initiative on tasks after having been given instructions, you will most likely be thought of as enthusiastic, courageous, creative, committed, and ambitious. You will also be helping your fellow workers by getting the job done."

2. *Voicing complaints and saying negative things:* "In the United States, managers like to know what is going on in the workplace, even if it is bad. A good employee keeps the manager aware of problems. Reasonable complaints are a sign of a cooperative, aware, and involved employee."

3. *Admitting lack of understanding:* "The employee who admits that he or she doesn't understand something is thought to be more concerned with getting it right, more enthusiastic, and more committed. You are not helping the manager by pretending; you are only creating problems that will surface later. If you pretend to understand, you might be thought of as dishonest and are risking making an error later that will create problems for everyone."

4. *Seeking and accepting promotions:* "You are perceived of as more confident and committed to the corporation when you seek promotions. It shows that you are involved with the job and is a signal that you have the ability to do it well. It is not considered in poor taste or disruptive of harmony."

5. *Praising oneself:* "Praising oneself shows confidence and ability. It aids the manager in that he or she can then make more informed decisions about hiring and promotions. This, in turn, helps the manager to do a better job and makes the entire company run more efficiently."

6. *Speaking English in the workplace:* "Speaking a foreign language in the workplace makes others feel left out and uncomfortable. It can also appear rude and unprofessional to colleagues, clients, and customers."

Explaining your perspective can be difficult. Your task will be simpler if you follow these guidelines:

- Think out carefully what you want to say.

- Conduct the conversation on neutral territory rather than in your office; this will be less intimidating.

- Use the written word; to do so will lend your message importance and give the worker an opportunity to discuss its content with colleagues and countrymen.

Additional suggestions for explaining your expectations will be found in the discussion of how to speak the worker's cultural language.

If you become frustrated, remember that your efforts are perhaps the first ones that anyone has made to familiarize immigrant workers with the expectations of you and your colleagues. Be patient and follow the guidelines on how to bridge language barriers in chapter 2; you will be amazed at the progress that you and your workers will make.

3) Compromise

Compromise is always possible even in the face of the most diverse cultural values and behaviors. Being willing to compromise is one of the primary ways in which respect can be shown and is also an effective means of encouraging cooperation and change.

This third step builds directly on the first in that it is impossible to devise successful compromises if the manager does not interpret the worker's motivations correctly. Based on the information gained thus far, jot down your ideas on what compromises might be made around our core behaviors:

1. Hesitance to take independent initiative on tasks

2. Reluctance to complain or make negative statements

3. Failure to admit lack of understanding

4. Reluctance to seek or accept promotions

5. Reluctance to praise self

6. Speaking of foreign languages in the workplace

Let us examine each of these and propose some compromises that might augment your own lists.

1. *Hesitance to take independent initiative on tasks:* One way to deal with this issue is to recognize that some workers are not comfortable with taking the initiative and compensate for this discomfort by telling the worker which specific tasks can be done without further orders. Another compromise might be to go further than you ordinarily would in giving specific instructions. By doing this, you will relieve the employee's anxiety about possibly making an error. Following up to make certain that everything is going smoothly and posting reminders on the bulletin board can also be helpful.

2. *Reluctance to complain and make negative statements:* A compromise here would be to say that complaints and negative

statements may be presented by the group as a whole, thus taking the responsibility off any one worker while honoring the value that is placed on the group over the individual. You might mention that complaints and problems could be represented to management by the informal group leader. This approach, too, will preserve the anonymity of the specific worker.

Another compromise is to use the suggestion box. In this way, workers can voice their problems without fear of appearing disrespectful or disruptive of harmony. Inviting complaints in private and reassuring workers that their anonymity will be honored are also helpful techniques.

3. *Failure to admit lack of understanding:* A similar compromise can be entered into when you want to encourage the admission that something has not been understood. Giving the worker the opportunity to voice confusion in private can greatly relieve the worker's concern that he or she will look foolish in front of others. Requesting that questions be put in writing is another compromise that will relieve embarrassment.

4. *Reluctance to seek or accept promotions:* Finding ways to compromise on this behavior can be a little more difficult. As we have seen throughout the book, there are many reasons that advancement may not be actively sought, and most of these reasons spring from deeply rooted values.

A compromise that might help would be to allow the process to take place through a third party—that is, encourage the worker to send a representative when asking for a promotion. Although this seems strange to the American manager, it is standard—harmony-preserving—practice in many other countries. Also, being discrete about the fact that an employee is being considered for a promotion will spare the candidate loss of face should his or her application be turned down.

Note: If you find you want to promote a worker who is not the informal leader of the group, you can avoid any tension by telling the leader what is going to happen. It is not that you are asking his or her permission but merely that you are compromising with the values of the group by acknowledging the leader's importance and position. To take it one step further, you might also allow the leader to make the announcement to the group.

5. *Reluctance to praise self:* Similar compromises can be made when encouraging self-praise. Making certain that interviews are conducted in private, allowing the worker to record his or her achievements and strong points in writing, or encouraging the participation of a third party are all helpful approaches. Other ways around this are to ask to see concrete evidence of what the worker has produced—a report, a proposal, a design of some sort, or even a physical object. Checking references, too, will take the worker off the hook as far as having to praise himself or herself.

Asking a series of specific questions that call for objective answers is helpful: "Tell me precisely what you did at your last job"; "Tell me about the role of the other members of your team"; "What part did you play on that team?"; "How would you handle a situation such as [hypothetical problem]?" The more concrete and objective the questions are, the more information you will gather.

Another technique is to ask employees what they think coworkers might say about their work. In this way, the self-praise becomes somewhat impersonal and, therefore, easier to express.

6. *Speaking foreign languages in the workplace:* This problem lends itself well to compromise. For example, invite the worker to speak his or her language in certain areas of the workplace and/or at certain times. Many corporations have found it useful to stipulate that speaking one's native language is encouraged as long as it is out of earshot of patients, clients, and customers. Allowing foreign languages to be spoken on breaks is another way of compromising on this delicate issue. You might also suggest that, if a foreign language is being spoken, the worker should mix it with English or turn to the native English speaker and translate.

Note: There are legal considerations around the issue of speaking foreign languages in the workplace—including the risk of discrimination suits. These concerns are complex and, in some cases, ambiguous. All managers and human-resource professionals should become thoroughly familiar with this aspect of the dilemma.

Another compromise around the language issue is for managers and colleagues to learn a few words of the worker's language. If we are able to say such commonplace expressions as "Good morning," "Have a nice weekend," or "Happy birthday," we are communicating both respect and a willingness to meet the worker halfway.

In the case of all these behaviors, the best way to establish an effective and permanent compromise is to ask the workers themselves. Inquire if they have any ideas about how they and the managers can meet halfway to make the workplace more efficient while still preserving the integrity of the employee's culture.

9) Speak the Worker's Cultural Language

Speaking the worker's cultural language is another way of communicating respect and thus increasing the chances of successful motivation. This means that you voice your request and the reasons for it in terms that can readily be understood in the context of the workers' cultural values and priorities. Cynics, for example, often say that members of mainstream American culture always understand the bottom line—that is, always respond favorably when a proposal is couched in terms of how much money it will make.

Loss of Face

Face saving is a central tenet of Asian cultures and, to a lesser extent, Hispanic and Middle Eastern cultures as well. The idea behind this value is that no one in a social or professional relationship should be embarrassed or humiliated in any way. The phrase *saving face* clearly constitutes an important piece of vocabulary in the cultural language of many immigrant or foreign-born workers. As such it can be used as a way of communicating your position in a fashion that will more likely be listened to and readily understood.

One of the reasons that the failure to take initiative, complain, or admit lack of understanding creates problems in the workplace is that each of these practices can cause loss of face for the managers and human-resource professionals. When the initiative is not taken on tasks, the job does not get done—a situation that reflects adversely on the manager's ability to supervise effectively. Similarly, if managers are left ignorant of problems in the workplace, they are incapable of fixing them and end up looking bad in the eyes of superiors and colleagues. Finally, if they are unaware that instructions have not been understood, there is no way they can remedy the situation and guarantee the smooth running of the workplace.

Reference to saving face can also be made as part of your efforts to encourage workers to seek promotions and praise themselves. You might point out that if they do not let you know of their qualifications, you will be unable to make correct staffing decisions and will lose face in the eyes of your superiors.

Loss of face also impinges on the issue of speaking a foreign language in the workplace. Explain that when a foreign language is spoken to the exclusion of others—superiors, colleagues, or customers—those who do not understand the language may feel left out, uncomfortable, and anxious, all of which result in loss of face and embarrassment.

Each of these cases involves a loss of face for someone. Since this value is so common to the multicultural workplace, it can be used when motivating behavior change. Not only will your request be quickly understood, but you will also be demonstrating that you cared enough to use a concept that the worker can relate to.

Respect for the Group as a Whole

Another bit of cultural language that can be used as a means of encouraging cooperation comes from the importance many cultures place on the group. Because of this priority, some workers are hesitant to seek promotions; they believe that to do so calls attention to the individual at the expense of the group. A similar rationale applies to self-praise; it is considered inappropriate and disruptive of group harmony.

One way to modify these behaviors is to point out that promotions and achievements reflect favorably not only on the individual but also on the group as a whole. The same argument might be made for the worker who does not want to take the initiative on tasks because he or she is concerned about standing out above the group. A response is to say that the group as a whole will benefit from any independent achievements of individuals.

5) Acknowledge Culturally Specific Needs

Becoming aware of and catering to culturally specific needs is the fifth step toward successful cross-cultural motivation. The difficulty is that we all tend to project our own desires and needs onto others and assume that everyone responds to similar rewards.

Exercise 5–3 demonstrates this problem. Take a moment to examine the list of motivators. Which ones do you think are desired throughout the world and which are specific to just a few cultures? Check the ones you feel are universal. Then rank the items according to their importance and value to you. In other words, how strong a motivator is each of them in your professional life?

As you can see, most of these motivators are what have been termed "soft currencies." Only financial gain and job security fall into the category of concrete external motivators.

This exercise serves two functions. First, by deciding which motivators are universal, you and your managers become aware of how few really are. Probably the only one of these motivators that is universal is social needs—the desire for human contact, comfort, and companionship. In Thai and Vietnamese cultures, for example, maintaining a positive relationship to others is the most powerful motivator of productive behavior. The rest of the list is specific only to certain cultures and, particularly, to Western industrialized societies.

Second, the exercise helps us to learn what motivates us so we can avoid projecting our own needs and wants onto others. You may have discovered that recognition, the chance to con-

---

Exercise 5–3. Identifying Universal Motivators

	Universal?	Importance to you
Recognition/respect	————	————
Responsibility	————	————
Financial gain	————	————
Social needs	————	————
Professional and personal growth	————	————
Advancement	————	————
The work itself	————	————
Power	————	————
Chance to contribute ideas	————	————
Chance to see concrete results	————	————
Job security	————	————
Autonomy	————	————
Structure	————	————
Chance to compete	————	————

---

tribute ideas, and advancement are particularly important to you. This would not be surprising because American culture values any forms of reward that single out the individual for attention. Praise, the prospect of a premium parking spot, a picture in the company newsletter, a prestigious promotion, or the title of "employee of the month" are widely sought by workers who were born and raised in mainstream American society. Indeed, Japanese managers who manage American workers marvel at how soon after being hired they seek promotions.

Competition, too, is valued in the West but considered disruptive of harmony and counter to productivity in many other countries. Even a monetary bonus, so highly valued in the United States, would bring humiliation to the Chinese, Japanese, or

Eastern European worker, who would feel that such a reward is in poor taste. We tend to forget that Western culture is largely unique in its emphasis on the material. When deciding how to motivate workers, look closely at what the individual employee really values and take care not to assume that all workers, from all cultures, value the same thing.

When deciding on incentives, managers should not neglect the offering of education and training as an effective motivation strategy. Education in the specifics of mainstream American culture, English-as-a-second-language training, and accent-reduction programs are valued by most immigrant workers and address the very specific needs of these employees.

The Value of the Family and the Group

The family and the group are of paramount importance within most immigrant and ethnic communities. This statement is, of course, a generality, but it serves as a guideline when trying to assess the needs and desires that are of greatest concern to your workers. It might be appropriate to motivate some Hispanic or Asian workers by offering them time off to return home for family events and holidays. The prospect of gala family gatherings and picnics can also constitute strong motivation, one that shows that you care enough about the worker and his or her values to seek out ways to satisfy those needs.

Related to the value placed on family is the wish to work overtime so as to be able to send money home to family, or to accumulate funds with which to bring family members to the United States. Allowing for the celebration of customary national holidays is another way of providing for family time while showing respect for the traditions of the group.

Job Security

Because many ethnic and immigrant workers share precarious socioeconomic status, job security often takes on great importance for them. The loss of a job can be a major tragedy for the individual and family alike. Reassure workers that as long as their work is good, they are in little danger of losing their jobs. Mention, in particular, that the behaviors you wish to encourage—initiative, negative statements, complaints, admitting lack of understanding—will not result in job loss even if the news is bad or an error has been made.

Verbal Acknowledgment of Needs

It is not always necessary or possible to meet every need you encounter in the multicultural work force. Sometimes it is enough to acknowledge that you know the need exists and that you respect a worker's right to feel that need. Acknowledging, for example, a worker's need for relaxation, companionship, and identity can diminish his or her desire to speak a foreign language while on the job. Sometimes just knowing our needs are understood can encourage cooperation and motivate behavior change.

6) Positively Reinforce Behavior

Providing positive reinforcement for the desired behavior is an important final step in any motivation process. Unlike negative reinforcement—criticism—which often leaves a worker feeling inordinately nervous and self-conscious and produces only short-term benefits at best, positive reinforcement, especially if emphasized in the early stages of a new behavior, can be very effective. Usually this is a simple matter: just notice that the worker is doing what you want and praise him or her for it. When it comes to motivating across cultural barriers, however, this step becomes a bit trickier. There are four problems to watch out for.

1. *Not all ethnic and immigrant workers are comfortable with praise.* This point has been emphasized repeatedly throughout the discussion. Many workers desire to avoid having attention drawn to the individual, are concerned about maintaining harmony and balance, and are preoccupied with social hierarchy and seniority. Another reason your praise might not get the

desired reaction is that compliments sometimes are accompanied by the implication that you are surprised that the worker did well. This is rather like the situation in which a colleague comes to work dressed particularly nicely and you react by exclaiming, "My goodness, you look good today!" leaving the impression that you are shocked and surprised that he or she looks so attractive.

The resistance to praise can be minimized by being discrete, using a third party or word of mouth, praising the group as a whole, putting a complimentary note in the worker's file, and being certain not to overpraise. Remember that fewer words are more effective, easier to understand, and less embarrassing.

2. *It is difficult to praise if an error has been made*. Mistakes will inevitably be made when employees take independent initiative on tasks. These errors present a great challenge to the cross-cultural manager who must correct the error while preserving the pride of the employee and continuing to encourage the taking of independent action. If pride and face are lost through an error, the chances of that employee's being willing to take the initiative again are slim.

The solution in this case is to treat the error as a separate issue from the initiative. You must point out the mistake, but at the same time you can put greater emphasis on how pleased you are that the worker had the courage to go ahead and act independently.

3. *It is difficult to praise when bad news is brought to you*. It is a natural human response to become angry with the person who comes to you with upsetting information. (The ancient Greeks used to execute the messenger who arrived with bad news.) It is understandably difficult, for example, for managers to bring themselves to praise the worker who arrives bearing news of a missed deadline or a broken piece of equipment. Managers should try to distance themselves from their distress long enough to praise the worker for keeping them informed and to encourage him or her to continue to do so.

4. *There is always the danger of taking certain behaviors for granted*. American managers are, for example, so accustomed to seeing workers take the initiative on tasks or seek promotions or

praise themselves during a performance review that it is difficult to remember that these are the behaviors that must be reinforced and encouraged with ethnic or foreign-born workers. The same applies to the speaking of English in the workplace. To speak English constantly can be a great effort, and yet it is a behavior managers are likely to take for granted. Try to stay aware of behaviors such as these. They seem automatic and commonplace to you but may be very difficult for the immigrant and ethnic employee.

Summary

Each of the six steps discussed in this chapter is important and useful. What they all have in common is the ability to help immigrant and ethnic employees adapt to the needs of American business while allowing them to maintain the integrity of their own cultural attitudes and values. To recap briefly:

- Provide reassurance to the worker that you are not trying to alter his or her culture.
- Understand the worker's perspective.
- Involve workers in decisions concerning the desired behavior change.
- Ask employees for ideas regarding compromises, and inquire how much they are willing to adjust.
- Help workers to feel psychologically safe and secure even in the face of change.
- Communicate respect for workers and their culture.
- Interpret behaviors correctly.
- Explain what you expect and why it is important.
- Compromise when possible.
- Speak your employees' cultural language.
- Meet workers' culturally specific needs.
- Remember that positive reinforcement is essential to successful motivation.

6
Cross-Cultural Management Training
Techniques and Pitfalls

All difficulties are easy when measure for measure they are known.
—William Shakespeare

This chapter covers:

- Information on how to assess your training needs
- Techniques for overcoming the manager's resistance to program content
- Tips on avoiding the pitfalls of cultural-awareness training
- How to choose the content of your cross-cultural management programs
- Format and exercise ideas

This chapter contains a great deal of personal opinion. After many years of speaking and training in the areas of cross-cultural management and communication, it is inevitable that one acquires numerous biases—biases about program design, strategy, and content. As human-resource professionals and managers, many of you are experienced trainers as well. You have your own training style, philosophy, and techniques. It is just such personal preferences that bring life and creativity to the design and presentation of any program. Do not allow my preferences to discourage you from bringing your own unique gifts to that process.

Establishing the Kind of Training You Need

Before spending any money, energy, or time on providing cultural-awareness training, it is important that you put some of these commodities into establishing the sort of training your organization needs. This step is especially important because there are many ways of approaching the challenges of managing the multicultural work force. Take the time to assess carefully which approach is appropriate for your managers and employees.

Is it really cross-cultural management training that you want? Maybe you need instead programs to help immigrant workers adapt to the American workplace. If management training is the issue, what level of manager should be trained? Do you start in the executive offices in order to gain support for the program or at the line-supervisor level so as to show immediate results? What ancillary training do you need: English language training? accent training? Is it really cultural diversity that is your problem? Maybe your difficulties have to do with personalities and are not related to culture at all.

Establishing your need is not always easy because you are dealing here with an issue that is subjective and difficult to measure. The following suggestions will help compensate for some of this subjectivity and allow you to get a clearer picture of how to proceed.

1. **Ask your managers, supervisors, native-born workers, and ethnic and immigrant workers how they feel.** Do this informally, without duress, and in confidence. Cultivate a conversational style so that the employee feels comfortable. The fact that you uncover a number of different opinions should not be disturbing to you. We know that cultural differences can create a lot of confusion. Differing interpretations of the same situation is just one manifestation of that confusion.

Carefully designed written surveys can be helpful, but beware of the so-called objective question that actually distorts reality. Personal interviews are safer and more accurate.

2. **Observe the workplace for yourself.** Lurk about, hang

out, and have faith in your general impressions. If you feel that there are misunderstandings, racism, or insecurity, there probably are. Are employees of similar backgrounds clustering and speaking their native language? How do the other workers react to this? Do people seem to be working well as teams, or is there conflict and bickering? Is the workplace running efficiently? Watch for these problems, and keep your eyes open for the subtle racial slur, "harmless" joke, or social slight.

3. **Study recent discrimination suits, complaints, disciplinary actions, exit interviews, employee assessments and reviews, new hirees, promotions, disability claims, and safety records.** These are concrete tools that can tell you a great deal about your workplace. What kinds of complaints are repeated? Do just a few managers or workers seem involved in the difficulties, or are they evenly spread throughout the organization? What particular cultures are involved?

Are certain groups of people quitting in inordinately large numbers? Are several leaving at the same time? If so, who are they, and why are they quitting? Examine your disability claims and safety records. Are workers getting hurt because they do not understand instructions?

4. **Invite a cultural-diversity consultant to do this appraisal.** There are times when an outsider can gather information more effectively than a company employee. Workers and managers might be less intimidated by this person and consequently more candid in their comments. Also he or she may have a more objective eye and be able to see the picture with less bias than someone who knows all the personalities. Having someone who is an expert in cultural diversity can also be an advantage because such a professional is aware of the kinds of cultural challenges that can arise and is therefore better able to spot them.

This is not to say that hiring an outside cultural consultant is always the best choice. There are problems too. Not knowing the personalities in your workplace can be an advantage, but it also can work against the consultant, who sometimes needs to know the history of each person in order to put his or her opinions and actions into perspective. Cultural consultants may have the disadvantage of being almost too preoccupied with culture. We become so immersed in the challenges of diversity that we develop a professional bias that causes us to interpret problems as culturally rooted when this might not be the case.

Whether to hire an outside consultant depends on the specific circumstances of your workplace. When making your decision, take into consideration the size of the work force, the complexity of the problems, the receptivity of employees, budgetary restrictions, and the availability of in-house staff who might be just as capable of conducting the needs assessment.

Selecting a Trainer

Your choice of trainer is perhaps your most important decision. Cultural issues are volatile and sensitive and require a person well versed in both the subject matter and the techniques necessary to diffuse conflicts and reduce resistance.

A trainer should have knowledge of the subject, speaking skill, sensitivity, the ability to field unexpected questions or criticism, a sense of humor, the ability to facilitate experiential interactions, and a knack for encouraging group participation. It is difficult to say which of these qualities is most important with respect to cross-cultural training; all seem indispensable. Certainly, however, the individual must have the courage to address the topic honestly and the awareness to avoid offending participants and workers.

Overcoming Participant Resistance

After you have identified your problems, established what you are trying to accomplish, and determined who you want to do the training, the next step is to confront any resistance that might be found among your employees. Cultural-diversity training is fairly new. Many managers look at it with skepticism and even anxiety. Many have never heard of it, and those who have are understandably concerned about the training and what it is trying to accomplish.

Some participants will be defensive. They will be thinking, "This is such a waste of time"; "Why do I need to learn about other people's cultures? This is America"; "I just know I am going to be preached at"; "I'm not going to change. I like the way we do things here"; "I've been a manager for ten years. I'll be darned if I'm going to change now."

These are natural reactions, especially since diversity training is new and managers have no idea what to expect. The process of diffusing this resistance begins long before the workshop actually takes place. It starts with titling and marketing the program with an eye to overcoming manager resistance.

If promotional materials for the training give the impression that attendees will be preached at, asked to do uncomfortable exercises, or told to give up their own culture, some changes must be made. Cross-cultural management training must be marketed as something that will provide managers with practical knowledge and techniques that will make their jobs easier. The other goals—improving teamwork, promoting harmony, reducing racism—will happen but only if the manager sees a personal benefit in the training.

If the program will be offered repeatedly to different groups of managers, first invite those employees who are likely to be the most receptive. These managers will be most easily impressed and, if the workshop is properly designed, will leave the program anxious to spread the word about how good, valuable, and nonthreatening the program is.

When the workshop begins, the process of overcoming resistance starts in earnest. At the very outset, the trainer should call attention to the fact that there may be resistance. If the attendees have been mandated to come, make light of it by saying that you know the group is there not because they are burning to learn about cross-cultural management but because their bosses insisted they show up. Lightness immediately dilutes some of the tension and puts the participants on the trainer's side.

The trainer should be clear from the start that he or she is aware of the specific cultural-diversity problems the trainees face. A few minutes might be spent outlining the difficulties that the trainer's research has turned up and then inviting the managers to identify any that the trainer might have missed. This time is well spent; it reinforces the fact that the program is for the managers and that they are there to get their own specific needs met.

At this point, you may notice that individual group members are hesitant to voice their problems in front of the other trainees. Our culture has taught us that it is wrong, or at least dangerous, to comment on differences among groups. This is doubly true when it comes to raising problems that arise from these differences. The instructor can eliminate this discomfort by bringing up a couple of examples of his or her own. They might be ones of a particularly sensitive nature—personal hygiene, food odors—that will give the message to the managers that it is all right to discuss whatever they wish.

Once participants have shared their difficulties, every effort should be made to address them. Too often trainers ask for specific problems, list them on a chart, and then proceed to ignore them throughout the program. Although it must be made clear that time will not allow every problem to be addressed, enough issues should be discussed so that the managers feel that they have truly been listened to.

In chapter 5, I emphasized the importance of making the culturally different employee feel psychologically safe to make adjustments by telling the worker that no one is trying to take away or change his or her culture but merely to change specific behaviors that are creating problems on the job. The same principle applies to the cross-cultural management workshop. By reassuring participants that they will have the opportunity to express their own views, in essence, to defend themselves psychologically, they become automatically more receptive. Invite the participants to be candid. Give them the opportunity to express their own feelings, however negative, regarding the problems and groups being discussed.

In order to sustain this feeling of psychological safety, the trainer must never imply that the manager has no right to feel the way he or she does about a particular issue. Of course, the workshop will provide information designed to dispel any negative feelings, but no stated judgment is made on the person holding these views. If participants are allowed freedom of expression, they will not be backed into a psychological corner from which their only defense is to resist any new ideas.

Another way of breaking down resistance is to focus on your managers' positive actions. Often training, particularly in areas that might be categorized as psychosocial, zeros in on problems. This approach invariably makes people resistant to what you have to say and is especially true if the manager has worked diligently to learn to do his or her job effectively.

Focus on what is right as well as what is wrong. Point out, for example, that the manager's instincts, honed through experience and exposure to different personalities, will serve him or her well in the multicultural workplace. By looking at what is going right, as well as what is yet to be mastered, the manager is given a feeling of competence and is encouraged to learn the new material.

Along this line, make it clear that, although culture is complex and subtle, some of the solutions to the challenges found in the multicultural workplace are simple. Using last names, taking time to chat, writing instructions down, and learning a few words of the language are just a few examples of the many powerful, and yet small, changes that can have an impact far out of proportion to the effort.

The final way to minimize resistance is to make the workshop lighthearted and fun. This does not mean to spend a lot of time playing games with no purpose but to set a tone from the start that the participants will not be preached at, that their way of life will not be threatened, and that the study of cultural diversity is fascinating and enjoyable.

How this lightness is created depends on the trainer's skill and personality. Some people bring an automatic playfulness to all training; others might have to rely on jokes, cartoons, or a couple of short, playful exercises to start things off. Continue this lightness throughout the workshop. If the program lasts all day, make certain that the playfulness continues into the afternoon when trainees may feel fatigued and overloaded with information.

Remember that cultural diversity is interesting; it tells us a lot about ourselves and about human relationships in general. It is a fascinating subject, and if the trainer is excited by it, the participants will be too.

Avoiding Offending Participants

Now that you have overcome any resistance to your program, both at the marketing stage and in the training room, you are ready to address a difficult question: How do you keep from offending people during the workshop? It is this danger of offending workers and managers of diverse cultural backgrounds that for many years has kept corporations from committing to badly needed cultural-awareness training. The unfortunate truth is that no matter how many precautions you take, there is always the danger of offending employees through the careless statement of a generality or the insensitive allusion to a controversial issue.

Programs of this nature contain a large quantity of ethnographic dynamite, which is in constant danger of exploding. As difficult as it may seem to avoid igniting some of this explosive material, there are a few techniques that can help the trainer conduct a program that is at once honest and inoffensive.

The first suggestion deals with the inevitable generalities any trainer is forced to make. Statements such as "Asians won't praise themselves" and "Russians don't smile as much as Italians" carry with them three risks. First is the danger that such statements might be misconstrued as applying to all members of a particular group—an obvious error in fact. Second is the risk that because participants intuitively know that such generalities are inaccurate, they will become skeptical about the trainer's ability to depict the group's cultural background accurately. Third, and most important for our purposes, there is the danger that such generalities will offend participants of that particular heritage.

What can be done to avoid offending someone because of a generality? It would be tedious to stop at every statement and declare, "This trait does not apply to every member of the group but is merely a generality designed to give you an indication of what you might encounter in the multicultural workplace." The answer lies, instead, in making one blanket disclaimer at the beginning of the program. A simple statement, similar to that found in the Introduction to this book, will do the job and, if stated clearly, minimize the danger of bringing offense to anyone.

A second way to avoid offending participants is to encourage extensive and spontaneous class participation. Give the group permission at the start to speak up if they hear something that offends them or if something is said with which they do not agree. This invitation should be stated within the first few minutes of the program and might be accompanied by the trainer's admission that he or she has much to learn from the audience and welcomes comments arising from their personal knowledge and experience.

Inviting dissension and disagreement serves not only to diffuse bad feelings but also sends the message to the group that the trainer has respect for them—for their views, their knowledge, and their ethnicity. Further, by requesting diverse opinions, the trainer has given the participants a feeling of control, an important precondition to the learning process.

Note: A fringe benefit of inviting participants to disagree with generalities is that such comments reinforce for the entire class the important point that every generality is inaccurate and that no one characteristic applies to all members of a group.

Misconstrued generalities are not the only way in which participants might become offended. The act of constantly analyzing, probing into, and focusing on specific cultures can make members of those groups feel as though they are under a microscope. One way to avoid this hazard is to discuss not only the cultures of immediate concern but others as well. Spread the attention out evenly. In particular, compare the behavior of other cultures to that of mainstream America. Do not be afraid to poke a little fun at the dominant culture. It is easy to do and is a lighthearted way of taking the pressure off the groups being examined closely.

Designing Program Content

Above all else, the program, whether it is offered by an outside trainer, by yourself, or by an in-house professional, needs to be tailored to the specific needs of your industry and your company. We have already looked at the steps that you might take to identify your most pressing problems.

There are also topics that ought to be an integral part of any workshop on cross-cultural management and communication. There should, for example, be a unit that defines terminology, such as *ethnic, culture,* and *culture shock.* Some time should be spent discussing stereotypes: what they are, what harm they do, and how they can be overcome. The issue of ethnocentrism and the dangers of projecting one's own culture onto others should also be discussed, along with an exercise or two to emphasize the point.

Beyond that, the course is up to you. The contents of this book can serve as a guideline to some possible subject areas. Are you concerned with motivation techniques or etiquette? Perhaps language diversity is creating problems in your workplace. Whatever the area, explore it thoroughly, encourage trainee participation, and utilize some of the exercises discussed in the rest of this chapter to emphasize the key concepts.

The design of a good program, however, involves more than just figuring out what issues to address. It is also important to establish a tone that closely matches the cultural style of your company and its employees. Should you choose, for example, to employ an outside trainer, insist that he or she acquire a good grasp of the personalities of those who will attend the presentation. Will they respond best to a program that is experiential? Will they prefer one that is more academic? Or is a basic nuts-and-bolts presentation more their style? What might their areas of resistance be? What are their specific problems? The tone or style of a program can be as important to its success as the actual content. This is especially true when dealing with a new and unfamiliar topic that is likely to be met with apprehension and resistance.

Making Use of Exercises

Exercises should accomplish something: illustrate a point, create an awareness, or practice a skill. With the exception of short devices that are intended merely to bring lightness and camaraderie to the training room, the exercises you choose should have a clear and practical purpose. Although this chapter devotes a lot of space to the topic of exercise design, bear in mind that exercises are only one component of a good workshop. Program content and group discussion should only rarely take second place to the use of these techniques.

When dealing with a difficult subject like cultural diversity, it is tempting to hide behind exercises that merely kill time or allow the participants to spend hours in fruitless play. Because of this temptation, every effort should be made to avoid being seduced by the latest game or experiential technique. Examine them closely, if possible see them in action, and ask some tough questions about the practical difference they make.

The amount of time and the types of exercises used in a particular workshop depend on a number of factors. What is the personality of your managers and the culture of your corporation? Is there a general liking of and receptivity to experiential learning, or is it frowned upon? You might also inquire into the personality of the trainer. Is he or she comfortable with and skilled at facilitating interactive learning, or is that process likely to seem stiff and forced? The amount of hours available has an impact on your choices as well. Exercises and experiential learning can take up a great deal of time. If time is limited, make your decisions carefully.

Another factor in determining your use of exercises is the particular needs of your managers. Did your initial needs assessment reveal that your managers require a lot of specific knowledge about different cultures? Are they lacking, for example, in information about varying cultural values and needs? If so, more time needs to be spent on teaching specific facts than in doing experiential work.

On the other hand, you may have found that the challenges

have more to do with communication skills and human relationships. Your managers may have a good grasp of the specific facts about their workers but are having difficulty relating well despite that knowledge. In a situation like this, experiential exercises in self-awareness, putting oneself in the worker's shoes, and communicating more effectively might be of greater importance.

The following sections present a sampling of cultural-awareness exercises. In addition, the "Training" section of the supplementary reading list contains a number of sources. Remember, too, that techniques designed for the teaching of other topics can often be adapted to the cross-cultural classroom. Use your imagination, explore the literature, and be creative.

You will notice that the categories are not distinct and that sometimes exercises from one group can be adapted to fulfill other functions. Although all of these ideas have been thoroughly tested, it is a good idea for you to try them on a small group before using them in your primary training. This extra step allows you to become familiar with the process and to anticipate any questions or difficulties that might arise.

Exercises

1. Warming Up and Getting Acquainted

Training books are filled with clever examples of how to warm up an audience and encourage participants to get to know one another. Many of these exercises can, and should, be adapted to fit the specific topic of cultural-diversity.

A couple of devices will illustrate the general idea; you can proceed from there to adapt your own favorite warm-up exercise to the cultural-diversity workshop. A simple and proved technique involves each participant choosing a partner whom they do not know and spending a few minutes sharing information about themselves. This procedure allows the managers to get to know someone new while they warm up to the idea of group discussion.

This exercise can be adapted to the cultural-awareness workshop by having the partners discuss something germane to the issue of cultural diversity—perhaps their own ancestry or country of origin, a challenge that they are facing in the multicultural workplace, or some of the advantages of having a culturally diverse work force. Another option might be that they discuss their own strengths and weaknesses in cross-cultural management.

A second well-known warm-up and get-acquainted game is what might be called Diversity Bingo. This is a game in which a bingo card is constructed with squares large enough to accommodate a number of signatures; twelve is ideal. In each square is printed a description or characteristic of a person. Before the workshop begins, each participant is asked to circulate and collect signatures of those who fit into each category.

Use your imagination with the categories. You might have the players find someone who was born in another country, speaks more than one language, is married to an immigrant, has worked overseas, has lived overseas for more than two years, or has ancestors who came to America before 1700. The options are endless and should relate as specifically to your own industry and company as possible. When the group reconvenes, establish who has the most signatures and give a prize. This exercise gets the group acquainted, encourages interaction, and, if the grid is constructed cleverly enough, raises some important issues about cultural diversity.

2. Diffusing Resistance

A technique for diffusing the resentment and resistance that some managers may feel when asked to come to a workshop on cultural diversity is to break the class into small groups and have them discuss their preconceived ideas about the program, their resentments, and their fears about it.

In the pages that follow, there will be many examples of various topics which can be discussed in pairs, in small groups, or with the group as a whole. In most cases, the choice of how to structure the discussion is a practical one which depends on the number of participants and the amount of time available. In this case, however, it is best to confine the discussion to pairs or small groups so that the comments will be more candid. If asked to vent their fears and complaints to the group as a whole, participants may be concerned about offending the trainer or appearing too critical and negative.

It is not necessary for the trainer to hear these comments but merely that the managers have the opportunity to express them. However, a trainer with good rapport with the class might call for anonymous reports back from the leader of each small group.

3. Focusing Attention

After the group has been warmed up and given the opportunity to voice their concerns, the next step is to focus the participants on the topic of the day. One approach is to have the group discuss, in either pairs or small groups, the specific challenges they are facing in the multicultural workplace. The idea here is that some managers might be aware of difficulties but need some help to figure out specifically what the problem area might be. It might be language, motivation, clustering, or any number of other issues. Often the simple act of being asked to verbalize a problem can allow the participant to organize his or her thoughts and clarify an otherwise muddled issue.

If this discussion takes place in small groups, you will need to allow time for each group to report back to the class. As the problems are raised, write them on a blank transparency or flip chart so that they will not be forgotten. An additional function of this exercise is to allow the trainer to focus on the topics of greatest concern to the managers.

A more structured way to accomplish this same task is to use a handout such as the sample found in appendix G. Entitled "What Do I Want from This Program?" this document lists a number of problem areas that will be covered in the workshop. Each list, of course, would be designed for a particular program. The participant is asked to rank these topics according to their importance for that individual. Space is provided in which additional concerns can be listed. After a few minutes, volunteers can share their most pressing, and least pressing, concerns with the group. These concerns might be recorded on a flip chart or transparency.

The function of these exercises is to encourage the managers to focus their thoughts on the areas that concern them most. In this way they can watch for the solutions to the specific problems they are experiencing. These techniques also serve to show the trainer which issues should be emphasized.

Another way to accomplish the same goals while making the point that there are many positive aspects to cultural diversity is to have individuals, pairs, or groups list the challenges and advantages of a multicultural work force. As these are shared with the group as a whole, problems are isolated, and in addition, people become aware of some of the benefits of a multicultural workplace.

A more personal way to focus the group on the topic and issues of cultural diversity is to ask people to write down or discuss their strengths and weaknesses when it comes to cross-cultural management, communication, and understanding. Perhaps each manager can ask himself or herself the question: "In cross-cultural management, I am most proud (and least proud) of my ability to . . . " Put more simply, the question might be: "When it comes to managing my multicultural work force, what am I good at, and where do I need improvement?" By asking these questions, the participants focus on their strengths and bring to the surface the areas in most need of improvement.

4. Pretesting

Pretests and posttests are useful evaluation tools that help establish the effectiveness of the training program. More important is the function they serve to accelerate the learning process. Pretests are an excellent way to pique the participants' interest. If cleverly written, they raise intriguing questions that promote enthusiasm for the program. They also have the power to encourage learning by showing managers that they, often very much to their surprise, know quite a bit about cultural diversity. This discovery invariably makes trainees want to learn still more. Even if the participant does not do very well, pretests can be motivating in that the trainees become aware of how badly they need the material to which they are about to be exposed.

A sample pretest is found in appendix H. Entitled "Cross-Cultural Awareness Assessment," it was designed for a specific client who had a particular set of difficulties. To make up your own test, figure out what you want to cover in the workshop, decide on which points are most important, and construct interesting, intriguing questions that address those points.

The reason that the pretest should contain well-thought-out questions is that this document is perhaps the first one that the manager will see after entering the training room. The questions it contains will influence his or first impression of cultural-diversity training. The following two questions deal with the same content, but one of them is more interesting than the other:

1. True or False: Americans maintain eye contact, on average, longer than any other major group.

2. Americans maintain eye contact, on average, for: (a) 1 second, (b) 10 seconds, or (c) 20 seconds.

The second question is more interesting than the first. This is because it contains a concrete fact that gets the manager thinking, generates discussion, and encourages people to ask themselves questions like, "How long do I maintain eye contact?" or "Is 1 second long or short?

Pretests should be scored, by the participants, before the workshop begins. For this reason, all questions need to have an objective answer and be either multiple choice or true or false. It is all right if there is more than one correct answer to some of the questions. Just make it clear to the trainees that this is the case. As with Diversity Bingo, a prize for the person with the best score can bring a playfulness to the process that sets the tone for the day.

Pretests and posttests do not have to be confined to the beginning and end of a workshop. They can break up the monotony of the day by being administered before and after units of particularly important content. Chapter 4, for example, contains a quiz entitled "Body Language: A Cross-Cultural Quiz" (exercise 4–2). Appendix I has a test entitled "Bridging Language Barriers: An Exercise in Awareness," which was designed to precede a unit on communicating across language barriers. Tests such as these can also serve to structure the content of the unit. In the latter case, for example, each question addresses an important issue on the topic of bridging language barriers. By going over a test such as this with the group and discussing each answer, the trainer can cover the essential material while simultaneously assessing the knowledge of the audience.

Another type of pretest is to give the group a case study to solve at the outset of the workshop. Undoubtedly the attendees will come up with some solutions but will not do as well as they would when the same case is offered to them again at the end of the day. What will happen, however, is that there will be a certain amount of frustration and anxiety—two emotions that educators know are preconditions to successful learning. By having the group attempt a task (solving the case study) that they are not quite capable of doing, they will be motivated to relieve this mild frustration by paying attention to the information supplied in the program.

Pretests and posttests should be creatively designed to generate interest. If you are particularly concerned that your managers learn the values of their Mexican workers, for example, you might structure the test around that issue, perhaps by stating a value or behavior and asking the managers how they think their Mexican workers would feel about that statement. For example:

Value: A good manager often asks workers for their opinion.

Question: How are most Mexican workers likely to feel about this statement? They will:

a. Strongly agree.
b. Agree.
c. Be neutral.
d. Disagree.
e. Strongly disagree.

This is just one example of a creative pre-test question. Use the material in this book to focus on the important issues and develop questions designed to test your managers' knowledge while piquing their interest in what you have to say. Whatever questions or format you choose, the same test can be slightly reworded and rearranged for use as a posttest in order to evaluate the amount of learning that has taken place.

5. Experiencing the Immigrant's Perspective

One important step toward effective cross-cultural management and communication is for managers to understand the emotions and perspective of the immigrant worker. Although the following suggestions are just exercises, they can conjure up "real" feeling and come close to making the immigrant's perspective clear to the manager.

The simplest way to accomplish this goal is to ask the managers, individually, in pairs, or in groups, to think about and/or discuss a time when they felt left out, different, or in the minority. This might have been when moving to a new school, when entering a new job, when walking through a primarily ethnic neighborhood, or when traveling abroad. Have them discuss not only what it felt like but how they reacted to it and the methods they used to cope with the situation.

Exercise 1–1 is one version. In it the reader was asked to write down how he or she felt under various circumstances, each of which simulated a different cause of culture shock. The result of devices such as this is that the manager is able to get some idea of how the culturally different worker feels when immersed in the American workplace.

Another example of this approach was used in the discussion of language differences when the reader thought about an experience in which he or she did not speak the dominant language. Here a series of four emotions were listed; loneliness, fear, passivity, and inadequacy. The reader circled a number that most closely reflected the intensity of that feeling.

In chapter 5, attempts were made to help readers understand how the immigrant worker feels when asked to behave in a way that does not fit with his or her values and cultural style (exercise 5–1). The manager who, for instance, was told never to seek promotions would certainly feel a confusion akin to that felt by the immigrant worker who is encouraged to brag about his or her achievements.

Another familiar technique used to elicit the same awareness is that of role plays. Role plays can be dangerous when dealing with cultural diversity, however. By asking one person to "play" a Korean or pretend to be a Mexican, you are risking stereotypical behaviors that could be embarrassing or offensive to others. One way around this difficulty is to ask for the characteristic behaviors to be acted out without labeling the group being portrayed. A further precaution is to have the role play conducted by all participants at the same time, not by one set of actors in front of the entire group. This anonymity is far less threatening and much less likely to make any one person uncomfortable.

The first step in this process is to have the group break into pairs. One of the pair arbitrarily is number 1 and the other number 2. The group is given a topic of conversation. The topic does not matter, but it does need to be something that lends itself to the asking of fairly personal questions. Written instructions are then given to each party as to how to behave while conversing with the partner. They are not to show their instructions to the other person.

Actor number 1 might, for example, be given these guidelines: "During this conversation, stand very close to 2, gesture boldly, maintain very direct eye contact, talk louder than usual, ask many personal questions, and interrupt when 2 is talking." These instructions are, in a very general way, characteristic of outgoing and flamboyant cultures. Actor 2 might be told, "Stand 3 feet away from 1, fidget with something, avoid eye contact, speak very softly, do not initiate any topics or ask any questions, show no emotion, smile shyly, and act generally uncomfortable and unresponsive." About 2 or 3 minutes is allotted to the conversation. The pairs then report back and share their experience with the group as a whole.

In terms of understanding what the immigrant or ethnic worker experiences, the partner who has been asked to behave shyly suddenly knows what it is like to be a soft-spoken Asian faced with the louder, more assertive American manager. And the aggressive partner becomes aware of how the more out-spoken immigrant feels when attempting to carry on a conversa-tion with someone who backs up, does not look him or her in the eye, and has little to say. This actor also soon discovers that when faced with an extremely soft-spoken partner, there is a temptation to become increasingly aggressive in a semiconscious attempt to get a reaction out of the other person. This is a valuable piece of information for the manager who works with large numbers of gentle, soft-spoken workers.

A second point that emerges from this exercise is that the participants begin to realize what it is like to be asked to behave in a style very different from their own. To be asked to speak louder or gesture a lot can be very uncomfortable for the person who is normally quiet and restrained.

What is it like to be an outsider or a minority who is dis-criminated against? Each of us has felt these feelings at some time, but there is nothing like immediate experience to drive the point home. The following exercises make this experience a bit more fresh in the minds of the majority manager.

One technique calls for the participants to form a circle, facing inward, and grasp arms. One person is arbitrarily chosen as the outsider who must try, by any means possible, to get inside the circle. The people who have formed the circle talk and laugh among themselves while doing everything they can to keep the outsider out. The exercise continues for 3 or 4 minutes. Debriefing consists of the outsider's comments on what it feels like to be excluded and the insiders' feelings about how it felt to be so exclusive. Questions are raised concerning the methods the outsider devised to break into the circle and how the insiders responded.

Similar insights are gained through the game of catch. Partic-ipants are lined up, and the facilitator begins to toss a ball to each person in the line. One person, however, is consistently excluded and has no chance to catch or throw the ball. After the exercise is over, that person is asked how it felt to be left out of the game, and the other players are invited to comment on the dynamics of what happened and how they felt about it.

These previous two exercises in which one person is singled out for exclusion take a bit of emotional toughness and they are not appropriate to all training settings. There is an alternative that might be a little easier on the more softhearted trainer. In this case, about one-third of the group is designated the "disadvantaged minority." This designation might be arbitrary, or it might be based on eye color, initials, make of car, or any other criterion.

After the group is divided into "minority" and "majority" managers, the minority is informed that they will be treated differently until the end of the first refreshment break, but they are given no clue as to what "differently" means. The majority managers are taken aside and told to ignore, boss around, and disagree with the minorities. Until the end of the exercise, the minority managers are ignored by the trainer, excluded from conversation by the majority, and generally treated with discourtesy and quiet disrespect. After the break, and probably very much to the relief of all, the exercise ends and the obvious ramifications discussed. The exercise is especially valuable if there is time to reassign the roles of minority and majority and go through the process once more.

6. Facilitating Cultural Self-Awareness

Managers need to become aware of the perspectives and feelings of their workers, but they also must become conscious of their own cultures and values in order to keep from projecting them onto others. Chapter 1 contains some examples of how to promote this cultural self-awareness.

One way to accomplish this goal is to have the managers write down three cultures with which they identify and then note three characteristics of each culture. A second method is to list proverbs, axioms, or idioms from U.S. culture and have the managers write down or call out the characteristics each entry represents. Alternatively, managers might construct their own list of proverbs along with the value associated with each.

The participant might also achieve cultural awareness by listing his or her own cultural values in one column and then coming up with ways in which those values are reflected in the trainee's behaviors. A somewhat simpler way to do this is for the trainer to provide the list of values and then invite the managers to fill in ways in which each value is manifested in their lives. An abbreviated version of this exercise might look like this, with the first two "Manifestations" filled in to illustrate the idea:

Value	*Manifestation*
Productivity	Hard work
Efficient use of time	Punctuality
Future orientation	
Change	

The purpose of this exercise is twofold: to help managers become aware of the culturally rooted values they hold and to allow them to think about how much that value is a part of their lives and, consequently, how much they are likely to project it onto the behavior of others.

A fourth way in which to encourage cultural awareness is to list the features of another culture and then have the trainee fill in his or her own version of that feature beside it. A short sample might look like this:

Asian Culture	*Manager's Culture*
1. Values the group over the individual.	
2. Prefers discrete, understated praise.	
3. Hesitates to question authority.	

You will notice that the right-hand column is labeled "Manager's Culture," not "U.S. Culture." This broad designation gives the trainee a chance to take note of the culture that most strongly dictates his or her attitude toward a particular value. In some cases, it may not be mainstream American culture but a regional, corporate, or ethnic culture instead.

An amusing exercise, and one that constitutes a fifth cultural-awareness exercise, is to ask participants to write a table of contents for a book on U.S. culture (or any other culture with which they deeply identify). You are inviting the class to author a list of chapter titles that reflect the basic characteristics of the culture. An example of a title might be, "Big, Bigger, Biggest" to represent the value placed on size and quantity in the United States, or "Don't Let the Grass Grow under Your Feet" to illustrate the importance placed on constant mobility. This is a good way to accomplish this important task and can also allow the trainees to get to know one another in a playful atmosphere.

A sixth approach is to compose pairs of statements, with each pair representing a different culture's attitude toward the same issue. Ranging between these statements would be numbers indicating how much the manager agrees with either position. The following abbreviated samples illustrate the idea:

1. We can control the future.   1 2 3 4   Fate controls most things.

2. Competition aids productivity.   1 2 3 4   Competition leads to disharmony.

3. Youth is most valuable to society.   1 2 3 4   The aged are most valuable to society.

The participant circles the number that best represents his or honest feelings (1 indicates strong agreement with the statement on the left, 2 mild agreement, 3 mild agreement with the statement on the right, and 4 strong agreement). You will notice that there is no middle-of-the-road number that allows the person to take no stance. Another example of this exercise can be found in chapter 3 (exercise 3–2) under our discussion of "Valuing the Whole Person."

An interesting twist can be added in this exercise by having the trainees add up the numbers they have circled and divide the total by the number of pairs of statements. The resulting figure will indicate (in the most unscientific manner possible) how attuned the manager is to either of the cultures.

7. Promoting Stereotype Awareness

Becoming aware of our stereotypes is a key to reducing their ability to distort our perceptions. One way to accomplish this is to write down the first thought that comes to mind about a population group and then to note the source of that information. Did the stereotype get picked up in school, was it from television, or did it actually come from extensive experience with the cultural group in question?

After the participants have completed their responses, have them share their lists with a partner to see how similar they are. This exchange often produces enlightening discussions about how different our perceptions can be of the same group and how unreliable our sources of information usually are.

The last step in this exercise is to have volunteers share their lists with the entire class. Despite the often sensitive nature of these revelations, many managers are prepared to reveal even very negative responses. Those who volunteer to read their stereotypes are usually aware on some level that their prejudgments are inaccurate and that the underlying source for that prejudgment is unreliable (the media, an isolated incident, rumor), and they often express the wish that they felt differently.

A second exercise to facilitate the identification of stereotypes has participants write down the stereotypes they hold about any group they wish. The group does not have to be one discussed in the workshop as long as it is a population about which the manager has strong ideas and prejudgments. The participant is reassured that his or her comments are written in complete privacy and will never be seen by anyone else.

After talking for a few minutes about the importance of recognizing our stereotypes for what they are so that we can discard them, the trainer asks the participants to crumple, tear up, or shred their comments. The trainer then moves through the room with a paper bag into which the papers are tossed. The purposes here are to identify the stereotype and to illustrate how important it is to set those ideas aside.

8. *Experiencing Other Kinds of Self-Awareness*

Becoming aware of one's own culture and the stereotypes we hold are only two of the many areas of self-awareness that can be helpful in our cross-cultural interactions. This book offers several examples of techniques designed to encourage various types of cultural awareness.

Exercise 4–1, for example, helps managers become attuned to how sensitive they are to cultural variations in etiquette and how they react emotionally under different circumstances. The same insights can be gained through providing short case studies or simple descriptions of behaviors and asking participants to comment on how they respond emotionally to such behaviors. Statements like "When an Asian workers fails to go after a promotion when I know he wants it, I feel . . .," or "When a Hispanic man holds my lapel while talking to me, I feel . . ." are good examples of the kinds of open-ended statements that can lead to self-understanding.

Either of these formats can be used for a number of other cultural issues like negotiation strategies, communication styles, or attitudes toward authority. Any of the material covered in this book could be adapted to just such an exercise. No matter what the specific content, the purpose of this format is to create an awareness of how the manager feels about and responds to a particular behavior. This awareness, in turn, will allow the manager to short-circuit excessive responses and devise instead reactions and interventions that are more moderate and productive.

A third way in which to achieve the same goal is to call upon the manager to construct an internal dialogue in response to a case study. This case study might be one which you have prepared or an incident that the manager has recently experienced. In any case, the scenario should represent some sort of a challenge in cross-cultural management. After reading or composing the case, the managers write down their initial emotional reaction to the incident. They then counter that first response by recording a more rational alternative reaction. A trainee might, for example, have recently encountered a worker who performed a task incorrectly because he was too embarrassed and afraid to ask for further instruction. The manager's response and internal dialogue might look something like this:

First response: I feel like this fellow is very lazy and stupid. All he had to do was ask. He obviously doesn't care about his job.

Rebuttal: Actually, now that I think about it, he does work awfully hard and has never missed a day of work. He must care about his job. I've noticed his English isn't very good. Maybe he figured that he wouldn't understand the instructions even if he asked.

The dialogue can be as elaborate and lengthy as you like, but even a simple one-statement reaction and rebuttal can lead to insights that can be readily applied back in the workplace.

9. Assessing Past Behaviors

The exercises in this section are designed to get a grasp not just of the manager's feelings but of his or her behaviors. What we are after here are current and past responses to particular intercultural challenges. One immediate benefit of exercises such as these is to boost the manager's confidence by calling attention to incidents in which he or she handled a cross-cultural encounter successfully.

The class is divided into groups or pairs, and each participant is invited to share an incident in which he or she succeeded in solving a culturally rooted problem. This sharing is especially valuable because the other members of the group learn from the speaker's success. Additional interest can be brought to this interaction by having members of the small group vote on which resolution was the most impressive or creative. A spokesperson for the group could then share the winning case with the class.

A variation on this exercise is to have participants share

difficulties in which their solutions did not work. Fellow group members can then try to figure out how the situation might better have been resolved.

A second way to promote awareness of past and present actions is to list behaviors and then ask participants to note how often they actually practice those behaviors. For example:

1. I make certain to pronounce my employees' names correctly: Always/often/sometimes/seldom/rarely/never.

2. I take the time to talk with my Mexican workers: Always/often/sometimes/seldom/rarely/never.

In addition to its primary function of assessing the manager's behavior, this exercise serves to emphasize some of the key points of the day.

10. Designing Case Studies and Critical Incidents

Case studies or what have been called "critical incidents" can be used for many purposes: as a pretesting device, as self-awareness tools, as gauges of past behavior, and, most important, to promote the learning process.

One of the good qualities of case studies is their flexibility. They can be a variety of lengths—from a single descriptive statement or question to a lengthy, complex scenario. Case studies are also flexible in terms of how they are used; their applications are limited only by the trainer's imagination.

The simplest type of case study is a narrative containing a problem to be solved or a dilemma to be analyzed. Individuals, pairs, or small groups are then invited to solve the problem or sort out what the characters did to create their dilemma. This approach has the advantage of allowing the participants to be creative and often produces insights that even the instructor had not thought of. It also lends itself to unstructured brainstorming sessions in which ideas are freely and uncritically tossed out by members of the group.

If the instructor's goal is to focus the trainees' attention on specific issues, a series of questions could follow the case study. Some suggested questions might be: What mainstream American and immigrant values are reflected in this incident? How might this problem have been avoided? How would you have behaved under these circumstances? Do you agree with the way in which the problem was solved? If so, why? If not, why not? What do you really know about this situation, and which of your conclusions are based on mere assumptions?

A more structured approach is to have an incident followed by a point scale on which the participant indicates how much he or she agrees with how the incident was resolved by the characters. The following sample will give you the idea.

> Deborah supervises many Filipino workers. She likes them very much, and they are good employees, but she recently has begun to sense that there is dissatisfaction among them. In order to solve this difficulty, she decided to get straight to the root of the problem. She invited a number of the more senior Filipinos into her office and asked them directly what was wrong. When they avoided the subject, she probed deeper by asking questions like, "What are your personal feelings about this job?" "Does this job fit with your heartfelt goals and dreams?" and "Is there anything that I am doing as a manager which is making this problem worse?"
>
> How do you feel about Deborah's solution?
>
> Agree   1   2   3   4   5   6   7   8   9   Disagree
>
> Explain why you feel the way you do and what alternatives there might be.

Another option is to follow case studies or critical incidences with multiple-choice questions. This book contains many examples of this format (see chapters 2 and 3). If you use multiple-choice questions, try to make the options subtle. Some of them should be right, some wrong, some ambiguous, and some subject to debate. Well-written questions get the trainee thinking and generate lively discussion.

The following is a good example of a brief, well-designed, critical incident:

> You need to discipline a Vietnamese employee who has been in this country for some years, but who still adheres strongly to Vietnamese culture. The worker is male and is ten years older than you. What sorts of techniques would you use to make the process as productive as possible?
>
> a. I would pad my criticism with elaborate compliments.
>
> b. I would state the problem in softened terms.
>
> c. I would take care not to sit too closely to the worker.
>
> d. I would criticize the Vietnamese workers as a group and not single out the individual employee.

As you know from reading this book, some of these answers are not as straightforward as they appear. Option a, for example, is ambiguous. It is a good idea to pad negative comments with positive reinforcement, but how might the Asian discomfort with exaggerated or insincere praise affect your actions?

When composing case studies, keep in mind that the content and theme of each incident should relate specifically to the environment in which your participants work. Hospitality workers, for example, will learn a great deal more from a case set in a hotel than from an incident that takes place in an electronics firm. If possible, carry this specificity one step further and draw on your own experiences or on experiences recounted to you during the needs assessment interviews. The latter, of course, would be told in strictest anonymity. The closer to home that the case studies are, the more energy will be put into solving them.

An alternative to having the trainer compose case studies is for small groups to make up their own and then trade them with other groups for the problem-solving sessions. This technique forces each group to define their own problems carefully and provides the opportunity for those problems to be solved by the fresh perspective of other trainees.

11. Miscellaneous

The literature of training is filled with techniques that can be adapted to address the many aspects of cross-cultural communication and management. Following are just a few of those that can be particularly helpful in adding to the value of cultural-awareness workshops.

A classic exercise that adapts well to cross-cultural training can be used to illustrate the fact that we are largely blind to our own culture primarily because we are so close to it. This is an exercise called Count the F's. Project the following sentence, in this exact format, onto a screen and have the participants count the number of "f's" in the passage.

> FEATURE FILMS ARE THE RE-
> SULT OF YEARS OF SCIENTI-
> FIC STUDY COMBINED WITH
> THE EXPERIENCE OF YEARS.[1]

After the participants have been given a few moments in which to count the number of f's, the facilitator asks for a show of hands as to who sees three f's, four f's, and so on. The correct answer is six, but very few people ever read that many because there is a tendency to ignore the f's found in *of*. This is because the word *of*, like our own culture, is so familiar to us that we are in danger of ignoring it.

Another exercise makes the important point that we see what we expect to see. This relates to the danger of distorting our perceptions of human beings in order to fit a previously held stereotype. Project on a screen the following three phrases, again exactly as shown, and ask the audience to read what they see.

ONCE	PARIS	BIRD
IN A	IN THE	IN THE
A LIFETIME	THE SPRING	THE HAND²

Invariably the participants largely ignore the extra *a* or *the* in each phrase. This illustrates the human predisposition to normalize things so that they fit with previous expectations.

This principle can be demonstrated with an auditory exercise as well. A volunteer is asked to count from 10 to 1 backward. Most likely, the volunteer will begin to count "10, 9, 8," not realizing that he or she was asked to count *backward* from 10 to 1, which means to count from 1 to 10. The listener expected to be asked to count from 10 to 1, so that is what he or she heard. These two simple techniques demonstrate that we need to be careful to observe every incident and person with fresh eyes and ears so as to perceive and evaluate each accurately.

One of the points made in the discussion of foreign accents was the tendency for many of us to expect not to understand the speaker and, consequently, to stop listening closely—in essence to stop trying to understand. The "1–10" exercise could be used to demonstrate our poor listening habits. Another simple and entertaining exercise also serves to make this point. Ask the following riddles:

1. Is there any federal law against a man's marrying his widow's sister?

2. According to international law, if an airplane should crash on the exact border between two countries, would unidentified survivors be buried in the country they were traveling to or the country they were traveling from?

3. An archeologist claims he has dug up a coin that is clearly dated 46 B.C. Why is he a liar?

4. Is there a Fourth of July in England?³

You probably are not having a great deal of difficulty finding the trick in these questions, but that is because you are reading them. When heard instead, they are a great deal more difficult to decipher. You probably have figured out, for example, that only a dead man has a widow, that you do not bury survivors, that no one knew when the coin was minted that the date was B.C., and that there is a Fourth of July in England (it just is not celebrated).

As the participants answer each riddle incorrectly, they begin to realize that even under the best of circumstances, people do not listen very carefully. The trainer can carry the point further by pointing out that improved listening skills can greatly increase our ability to understand the nonnative English speaker.

In chapter 2, where we examined the issue of simplifying English, you will recall two exercises that emphasized the importance of keeping English simple and straightforward. Exercise 2–2 asked the reader to spot the idioms, jargon, and slang in a passage. The other (exercise 2–3) was to rephrase unclear passages into simpler, easier-to-understand verbiage.

The importance of keeping English simple might be emphasized by having managers reverse the process by taking a simple sentence and making it complex. In performing this task, the participant becomes more conscious of how he or she is prone to making sentences more complicated than they need to be.

12. Wrapping It Up

Posttests are an important form of wrap-up exercise. In some cases, they need to be objective and measurable for documentation purposes. If documentation is a concern, the simplest method is to use a true or false or multiple-choice pretest and then rearrange and/or reword it for use at the end of the program.

If your goal is not precise documentation but to solidify learning and get a general idea of how much has been accomplished, any number of the exercises outlined in this chapter could be used. You might present a case study to the group as a whole or to small groups for them to solve. Another technique is to ask the same questions used to assess managers' past behaviors, but this time ask how they would behave in the future having gained knowledge in the workshop.

Individually executed action plans are a good way to solidify the information learned and begin the process of applying it in the workplace. A sample action plan appears in appendix J. In this sample, the form calls for the names, or pseudonyms, of the individuals involved in the problem, the objective that needs to be achieved, the action to be taken, a deadline if appropriate, and a section in which to record the measures of success.

A final way to solidify what has been learned is to have participants call out the most valuable thing learned in the workshop. This takes only a few moments, helps the day to end on a positive note, and also lets the trainer know what information the managers felt was most important and worthwhile.

Some Practical Matters

The program should not be too long. Studying cultural diversity is fascinating but also hard work, especially if a lot of energy is being put into understanding new ways of looking at oneself and at others. Breaks should be frequent—every hour and a quarter, if possible—and the program should certainly run for no longer than 5 hours per day.

Bring as much variety as possible to the methods and media that you use. Mix discussion with lecture, videotapes, films, and group and individual exercises. Use lots of visual aids. If you use slides, keep the lights up as high as possible. A dimly lit room can make an audience groggy quickly. Be creative in your visual aids; use color, drawings, and even cartoons to illustrate points.

Because of the volume of material and its complexity, distribute lots of handouts. It is not necessary to go over all of these handouts at the workshop—that process can be extremely tedious—but merely to make them available for future reference. Published articles on cultural diversity and cross-cultural management, case studies with solutions supplied, tips on communication, motivation, conflict resolution, training, and interviewing techniques will all prove invaluable once the workshop is no longer fresh in the participants' minds.

Summary

Workshops on cultural diversity are not easy to conduct. There is always the risk of offending someone or of making dangerous and misleading generalities. But if you follow the guidelines laid out here, you can produce a program that will result in real and immediate improvement in the attendees' cross-cultural management skills. Here are the most important points made in this chapter:

- Take time to assess your company's needs.
- Use knowledgeable, sensitive trainers.
- Market the program carefully.
- Tailor the program to your managers' specific needs.
- Take time to diffuse resistance.
- Avoid making faulty generalities.
- Make your exercises count.
- Use visual aids and handouts.
- Encourage participation.

Notes

1. J.W. Newstrom and E.E. Scannell, *Games Trainers Play* (New York: McGraw-Hill, 1980).
2. Ibid.
3. Ibid.

Epilogue: Reaping the Rewards of Awareness

> Our fate is to become one and yet many—this is not prophecy, but description.
>
> —Ralph Ellison

I just found a penny on the floor of my daughter's room. Naturally I pocketed it, but before I did, I looked to see if the coin still carried the imprint, *E Pluribus Unum*. I was vaguely surprised to see that it is still there: *E Pluribus Unum* ("Out of many, one"). The idea of oneness out of diversity is central to American culture and to the values of our nation—so central that it continues to be indelibly stamped on millions of coins.

Perhaps this is because Americans have been adapting to and living with cultural diversity since long before the nation was founded. You might wonder how they could have adjusted so well without benefit of cultural-awareness workshops, inspirational speeches, and books on cross-cultural communication skills. How were they able to create, out of millions of immigrants and dozens of cultures, one nation composed of a rich assortment of peoples, each one of whom has added to the strength of the whole?

The answer is that our ancestors accomplished this remarkable feat with the aid of one essential tool: human instinct. In terms of relating to other cultures, this means the ability to be attuned to the commonalities that bind all peoples together—the basic human needs and nature that lie beneath the cloak of culture and ultimately allow us to understand one another.

Should you feel overwhelmed by the complexity surrounding you or begin to doubt your ability to apply your newfound knowledge, remember that you are blessed with the same instinct that served our forefathers so well. In addition, you undoubtedly possess many other natural skills and characteristics that will help you succeed in any culturally diverse environment. For one thing, you would not have opened these pages in the first place if you did not have a curiosity about the ways of others and a readiness to look at the differences between cultures. You also probably never would have bothered to pick up this book if you were not, to some degree, committed to the idea of cultural harmony and to the goal of making the most of your multicultural work force.

This same commitment also means that you have an open mind and a compassionate heart, and that you are prepared to adjust and adapt in order to bridge cultural barriers. I further believe that you are well qualified to develop successful intercultural relationships because you are already attuned to the importance of good communication skills. You care about people and see the value in understanding the perspective of those around you. In short, you already have the foundation of good relationships, whether they are between friends, within families, or between cultures.

It would not surprise me to discover that you have enough confidence in your own values and culture to learn about other ways of doing things without feeling threatened or defensive. This confidence means that you have the ability to continue being yourself while communicating respect for the ways of others. Finally, you probably would not have attempted to resolve your challenges in cultural diversity if you had not expected to succeed. Expecting the best in any endeavor is the first step toward fulfilling that expectation. Part of this optimism was expressed by Thomas Jefferson when he advised his readers to "take hold of things by the smooth handle"; that is, do not make any task harder than it actually is. Cultural diversity is complex, but within that complexity are many "smooth handles," many opportunities to take simple steps toward the goal of greater harmony and productivity.

Cultural diversity can be disorienting and confusing, sometimes even a bit frightening. If you approach the challenges of diversity with a spirit of adventure and optimism, if you expect to succeed and remember to keep your sense of humor, you will soon discover that understanding has replaced confusion and that your anxiety and fear have been magically transformed into excitement and curiosity.

Appendix A:
Foreign-Language Phrases

The following phrases are appropriate to use with immigrant workers. Each phrase has been rendered not in the language itself but in informal phonetic English to help you with the correct pronunciation. It is impossible for you to get the exact pronunciation by merely reading it on the page, but do the best you can; it is the effort that counts. Even if you do not do a very good job, your attempt to speak a few words of the worker's language will be appreciated and will be interpreted as a sign of respect. The key provided here will help you decipher some of the less obvious sounds.

Although every effort has been made to compile an accurate list, the complexities of language and the subtleties of pronunciation make some errors likely. This is particularly true of the tonal languages: Thai, Vietnamese, and Mandarin. In these cases, the meaning of words can change according to the tone with which the syllable is pronounced. Should you discover that you are making errors, ask for help from your immigrant workers and colleagues.

Not all of the English phrases have been assigned a foreign equivalent. This is because some of our greetings do not appear in other languages and would not be appropriate. In the Philippines, for example, one person does not wish another "a good weekend" because the weekend is not clearly distinguished from the rest of the week.

In some cases, alternative formal and informal ways of saying the same thing are provided. The choice of which to use depends on the nature of the relationship; the more intimate the friendship, the more informal the greeting. If you have any doubt about which to use, begin with the more formal. The worker or colleague will correct you if he or she would prefer the more casual phrasing.

Key to Pronunciation

a = "ah," as in *sock*.

à = the sound "uh," a staccato sound as if it were cut off in the throat.

aw = the "aw" sound in *saw*.

e = the "e" in *egg*.

ee = the "ee" sound in *see*.

eye = the "ear" sound in *bear*.

i = the "i" in *it*.

I = a sound like the pronoun *I* or the "ie" in *pie*.

kh = a very exaggerated "h." The closest thing would be almost like clearing your throat.

o = "oh."

oo = the "oo" in *boot*.

ow = the "ou" sound in *ouch* or the "ow" in *how*.

oy = the "oy" sound in *boy*.

rr = the trilled or rolled "r" used in Spanish.

r* = a guttural (French) "r."

u = the "u" in *pun*

uh = the "u" sound in *cup*. You will find this sound at the end of a syllable or word.

′ = Place the accent on the syllable or word indicated.

( ) = Parentheses surround any sound that is formed but is barely audible. This is a difficult concept for the English speaker to grasp. Do the best you can.

⌣ = a slurring connection between the two sounds.

Spanish

Good morning bwenos deéas

Good evening (when leaving work at the end of the day) bwenos noches

Hello ó la

Goodbye a deeós

Have a good weekend kay pásay oon felees feen day semána

Please por favor

Thank you gráseeas

Happy Birthday felees koomplayanyos

That's all I know [of the language] no say mas—es todo lo kay say

French

Good morning bo(n) joúr

Good evening (when leaving work at the end of a day) bo(n) swá

Hello bo(n) joúr

Goodbye or* vwa

Have a good weekend bo(n) weekénd

Please seal vou pláy

Thank you mer*sée

Happy Birthday bo(n) aniver*sair*e

That's all I know [of the language] say too suh kuh juh say

German

Good morning   goóten mórgun

Good evening (when leaving work at the end of a day)   goóten ábent

Hello   halo

Goodbye   owf véeder zayne

Have a good weekend   shóonus vókhun énduh

Please   bíttuh

Thank you   dánka

Happy Birthday   Say it in English; this phrase is commonly used and understood.

That's all I know [of the language]   dus ist allis vas ikh vus

Tagalog

Tagalog is the primary language of the Philippines.

Good morning   magandáng oomága

Good evening (when leaving work at the end of a day)   p à áh lam

Hello   koomoostá ka

Goodbye   pà áh lam (poetic and provincial); ba bye (informal, most often used)

Have a good weekend   This is not a phrase normally used in Filipino culture.

Please   pweday ba *or* pa kee (*Paki-* is actually a prefix added to verbs to distinguish them from commands. On occasion, it will stand alone.)

Thank you   salámat

Happy Birthday   Use the English; it is widely used and understood.

That's all I know [of the language]   yan lang ang alám kong ta ga log

Vietnamese

Good morning chao boóee san(g)

Good evening (when leaving work at the end of a day) chao tam be(t)

Hello chao ko (when speaking to a female); chao anh (when speaking to a male)

Have a good weekend chook koóee toong voóee ve

Please mooy moy

Thank you ka‿mon

Happy Birthday sinh ny(o)(t) voóee ve

That's all I know [**of the language**] toy chee b(e)(t) choo i(t) chay b(i)(t)

Khmer (Cambodian)

On the borders of Cambodia, Thai, Vietnamese, and Laotian are also spoken.

Good morning arróon sooe(r)sday

Good evening (when leaving work at the end of a day) leeyeh‿hI

Hello choom‿rreeapsóor

Goodbye leeyeh‿hI

Have a good weekend ban so(k) sabÍ naopel chó(b)somra(k)

Please sowm‿metá

Thank you aw‿kóon

Happy Birthday rrée rreeay tnI bon koob komna(d)

That's all I know [**of the language**] knyom man dan(g) tyetáy *or* knyom che neeyay tI boneh táy

Laotian

Good morning sabI dee

Good evening (when leaving work at the end of a day)   pI dee uh or nuh

Hello   chang dI

Goodbye   la kon *or* pI duh

Have a good weekend   sooksoon vanpak

Please   karoona (followed by the request in English or perhaps a non-verbal signal) *or* state the request first and follow it with: deh

Thank you   hob chI

Happy Birthday   sooksan van k(u)(t)

That's all I know [of the language]   hoy hoo pak pasa lao dI to nan *or* hoy hoo pak pasa lao dI to nee

Thai

Good morning   svat dee krap

Good evening (when leaving work at the end of a day)   pI dee krap *or* sok dee krap

Hello   yang ngI (informal)

Goodbye   la kon krap

Have a good weekend   sooksan vanpak

Please   karoona (fill in the request in English or perhaps a nonverbal signal) krap

Thank you   kob koon krap

Happy Birthday   sooksan vank(u)(t)

That's all I know [of the language]   pom (chan, if you are a female) rroo puut pása tI dI thao nee krap

Korean

Good morning   anyón(g) ha say yo

Good evening (when leaving work at the end of the day)   anyón(g) (You might add, if you wish: ha say yo.)

Hello   anyón(g)

Goodbye   anyón(g)

Have a good weekend   jó en jumál bo nay say yo (This is more closely "have a good day off." The weekend is not significantly different from the other days.)

Please   This is impossible to translate because there are numerous different phrases used for the concept of "please" depending on the context.

Thank you   kam sá ham ne dá

Happy Birthday   sang éel chuka hám ne dá

That's all I know [of the language]   ee go shé nagá a nun hangú(g) mal oóee zanbóo imnidá

Japanese

Good morning   ohio (like the state)

Good evening (when leaving work at the end of the day)   sIyonara

Hello   ko nee chee wa

Goodbye   sIyonara

Have a good weekend   yo ee shoo ma tsoo o

Please   do ood zo

Thank you   areegato

Happy Birthday   o tan jo oobee, o me de to oo

That's all I know [of the language]   wa ta shee ga shee te eeroo no wa, ko re da ke de soo

Arabic

Although there are several principle Arabic dialects, this is the one most widely understood.

Good morning   sabah al khéyr

Hello   sabah al khéyr

Goodbye   The person leaving says: allI saláynic. The person being left says: ma saláyma. (A very informal goodbye would be: ma alsalama. This amounts to "so long.")

Have a good weekend   Not applicable.

Please   mn fádluk

Thank you   shookrán

Happy Birthday   To a woman: kul es séna wintuh tIéebuh. To a man: kul es séna wintee tIéebuh.

That's all I know [of the language]   manaráfsh árabee áktar men he-thuh

Farsi

Farsi is spoken in Iran.

Good morning   sobh‿bekhéyr

Good evening (when leaving work at the end of the day)   shab‿be-khéyr

Hello   salóm

Goodbye   hóda haféz

Have a good weekend   veekende shomá hosh (formal); veekende sho-má bekheyr (informal)

Please   lotfan (formal); hawhesh mikohám (informal)

Thank you   mérsee

Happy Birthday   tavaló det moborák (informal); tavalode sho-má moborák (formal)

That's all I know [of the language]   man far*at hamin r*adr fársee midoonam

Mandarin Chinese

This is the most widely spoken of the Chinese dialects.

Good morning zow shang ha

Good evening (as when leaving work at the end of a day) wan shang ha

How are you? neen ha ma?

Goodbye sigh gee yen

Have a good weekend joe mor you quI

Please chin(g)

Thank you s(h)ee e s(h)ee e

Happy Birthday sung er quI la

That is all I know [of the language] je sure wha jer dah dee soy yo jung we(n)

Compiled by Elizabeth Mariscal and Krystyna Srutwa of SpeechCraft, and by Susan Montepio, Paco Sevilla, and Elizabeth Estes.

Appendix B:
Tips for Interviewing and
Assessing the Culturally
Different Worker

The following comments are amplified throughout the text. They are included here in abbreviated form to allow readers easy access to the most important points.

1. Do not prejudge a worker according to his or her ethnic background, name, or accent.

2. Do not draw rash conclusions from a gentle handshake, direct or indirect eye contact, or any other behavior related to cultural style.

3. Conduct the interview in private.

4. If culturally appropriate, allow workers to praise themselves in writing.

5. Examine physical evidence of past accomplishments, supply the applicant with a job-related problem to solve, and check references rather than insist on the worker's praising him- or herself.

6. Ask the applicant or employee what co-workers would say about his or her work.

7. Ask a series of questions in order to learn of past accomplishments.

8. Ask that the applicant complete the application in the office and alone as a means of checking English-language reading and writing skills.

9. Assess English-language reading skills by including some lengthy instructions on the employment application.

10. Assess English-language writing skills by asking for a short essay on the employment application.

11. Assess how much the worker speaks and understands English by involving him or her in a lengthy conversation.

Appendix C:
Cross-Cultural Criticism and
Coaching—Some Guidelines

Most of these tips are discussed in greater depth throughout the book but are included here as a quick review.

1. Remember that the effect of your criticism and evaluation is not confined to the immigrant worker's professional life.

2. Make it clear that you want to help.

3. Explain that everyone in the organization is coached and evaluated periodically.

4. Be aware of culturally sensitive areas.

5. If there is a problem, comment on it as soon as possible.

6. Be careful of body height and space.

7. Be aware of tone of voice, pace, and loudness.

8. Do not talk too much.

9. Criticize in private.

10. Inquire about cultural background.

11. Consider criticizing and coaching the group as a whole rather than the individual.

12. Show positive and negative outcomes of various behaviors.

13. State the issue as a problem, not as a criticism.

14. Criticize the action, not the person.

15. Be concrete and specific in what you expect.

16. Provide positive reinforcement of good work, but be careful not to overdo it.

17. Be courteous and, if appropriate, formal.

18. Use humor sparingly.

19. Discreetly inquire after the worker's personal welfare (for example, family and home life).

20. Listen carefully to the worker's perspective, and try to agree on the problem.

21. Communicate respect for the worker's culture.

Appendix D:
Diffusing Culturally Rooted
Conflicts in the Workplace

The following tips will help you identify and resolve conflicts that arise because of cultural differences in the workplace. These guidelines are applicable no matter which cultures are involved; this includes, of course, mainstream American culture.

1. Bring together the workers who are involved in the conflict (include informal group leaders if appropriate).

2. Give each party the opportunity to voice his or her concerns without interruption.

3. Attempt to obtain agreement on what the problem is by asking questions of each party and by finding out specifically what it is that upsets each person.

4. During this process, stay in control and keep the employees on the subject of the central issue.

5. Establish if the issue is indeed rooted in cultural differences by finding out:

   - if the parties are from different cultures or sub-cultures
   - if the key issue represents an important value in each person's culture
   - how each person is expected to behave in his or her culture as it pertains to this issue

- if the issue is emotionally charged for one or both of the parties
- if similar conflicts arise repeatedly and in different contexts

6. Summarize the cultural differences that you uncover.
7. State the negative outcomes if the situation is not resolved (be specific).
8. State the positive outcomes if the situation is resolved (be specific).
9. Negotiate terms by allowing those involved to come up with the solutions.
10. Provide positive reinforcement as soon as the situation improves.

Appendix E:
Training the Immigrant
and Ethnic Worker

The points listed below are discussed in several contexts throughout this book. They are included here for easy reference.

1. Do not try to cover too much material at one time.

2. Organize your thoughts, and avoid unnecessary asides.

3. Allow self-graded quizzes.

4. Avoid the use of multiple-choice questions.

5. Allow questions to be asked anonymously and in writing.

6. Invite informal group leaders to participate and ask questions as a way of encouraging the others.

7. Use visual aids.

8. Use extensive handouts.

9. Speak slowly and distinctly, but do not patronize.

10. Use simple phrasing and familiar words.

11. Avoid jargon, slang, and idioms.

12. Provide a glossary of necessary jargon.

13. Do not talk too much.

14. Recap and check for understanding frequently.

15. Do not force debate and competition.

Appendix F:
Cultural Contrasts

M ainstream American culture has certain perspectives that contrast with those found throughout much of the rest of the world. The following list is designed to depict these contrasts. Obviously no one attitude is held by every person within either group, nor does the "contrast culture" category take into consideration the nuances of individual cultures.

1. *Control versus fatalism*
   U.S. culture: Individuals have the power to control the future.
   Contrast culture: The future is influenced by fate or by a higher power. Seven-eighths of the world's population believes in fatalism.

2. *Control of nature versus harmony with nature*
   U.S. culture: Nature can, and should, be controlled and used to meet human needs.
   Contrast culture: Humans are part of nature and should disturb it as little as possible.

3. *Change versus tradition*
   U.S. culture: Change is usually good.
   Contrast culture: Change should be resisted unless there is an obvious good to be gained from abandoning tradition.

4. *The importance of the future versus the past and present*

U.S. culture: It is important to plan for and anticipate the future.

Contrast culture: It is important to remember the past and enjoy the present moment.

5. *Reality is orderly versus reality is disorderly*
U.S. culture: All reality can eventually be categorized and ordered.

Contrast culture: Reality is chaos and cannot be objectively organized.

6. *Guilt versus shame*
U.S. culture: Acts are to be avoided out of fear of internal feelings of guilt.

Contrast culture: Acts are to be avoided out of fear of public shame.

7. *Unlimited versus limited supply of "good"*
U.S. culture: There is an unlimited supply of benefits and good things to be acquired in the world.

Contrast culture: There is just so much "good" to go around.

8. *Materialism versus spirituality*
U.S. culture: Acquiring material wealth is a sign of success.

Contrast culture: Spiritual growth is more important than amassing wealth. Material possessions can sometimes be a sign of poor spiritual health and can be disruptive of society.

9. *Practicality versus aesthetics and emotions*
U.S. culture: Practicality and pragmatic ends are more important than emotions or aesthetic considerations.

Contrast culture: Aesthetics and emotions are at least of equal value with practicality.

10. *Rational versus intuitive thinking*
U.S. culture: The most productive thinking is linear, cause and effect, and rational in nature; it is based on concrete evidence and facts.

Contrast culture: Intuitive, creative thinking is most highly valued.

11. *Quantification versus quality*
U.S. culture: Quantity and size are valued and considered the best way to determine success. "Best," "biggest," "jumbo," and "I feel like a million" are common expressions.
Contrast culture: Quality is the way to determine success.

12. *Becoming versus being*
U.S. culture: People should constantly strive to become better.
Contrast culture: There is value in simply existing as one is rather than constantly striving to become something else.

13. *Speed and time as priority versus time as secondary*
U.S. culture: Efficiency, scheduling, punctuality, and speed are of paramount importance.
Contrast culture: Units of time are undifferentiated and are only rarely an important consideration.

14. *Efficient use of time versus human interaction*
U.S. culture: Time should not be wasted on unnecessary conversation and social niceties.
Contrast culture: Time should be taken to build solid relationships, especially before doing business.

15. *Transient versus lifelong friendships*
U.S. culture: Friendships can be formed very quickly and dissolved just as fast.
Contrast culture: Friendships are formed very slowly but, when formed, last a lifetime.

16. *Youth versus age*
U.S. culture: Young people are valued and the elderly discarded.
Contrast culture: Age is to be respected.

17. *Individual versus group identity*
    U.S. culture: People gain identity from their individual achievements.
    Contrast culture: Individuals derive their identity from the family, company, or group.

18. *Individual versus group welfare*
    U.S. culture: Individual welfare and achievement is more important than the good of the group.
    Contrast culture: Group welfare and achievement is more important than individual accomplishments.

19. *Individual versus group decision making*
    U.S. culture: Individual decision making is often the most efficient method to use.
    Contrast culture: Important decisions should be made by the group, not by the individual.

20. *Independence versus dependence*
    U.S. culture: It is unhealthy to be dependent on family and the group.
    Contrast culture: It is proper to remain dependent on the family and group into and throughout adulthood.

21. *Self-Help versus birthright*
    U.S. culture: Position in life is achieved through individual effort.
    Contrast culture: Position in life is achieved through family heritage and connections.

22. *Questioning versus respecting authority*
    U.S. culture: It is all right, even desirable, to question authority figures.
    Contrast culture: It is wrong to question any authority figures.

23. *Persuasion versus compulsion*
    U.S. culture: The best way to get people to act is through persuasion.
    Contrast culture: The best way to get people to act is through compulsion and authoritarian means.

24. *Truth is debatable versus truth is absolute*
    U.S. culture: Truth is flexible and can be debated with managers, teachers, and authority figures.
    Contrast culture: Truth is absolute and should not be questioned.

25. *Achievements versus character*
    U.S. culture: Individuals are valued according to their external achievements.
    Contrast culture: Individuals are judged not according to their external achievements but by their general character and inner self.

26. *Equality versus hierarchy and rank*
    U.S. culture: Equality is to be honored.
    Contrast culture: Society is better organized if there is rank, status, and hierarchy.

27. *Complaints versus reluctance to complain*
    U.S. culture: It is all right, and desirable, to a point, to complain to one's superiors.
    Contrast culture: It is defiant of authority to complain to superiors.

28. *Boasting versus modesty*
    U.S. culture: It is appropriate to speak of one's own achievements.
    Contrast culture: It is disruptive of harmony and social balance to praise oneself.

29. *Risk versus face saving*
    U.S. culture: It is all right to take chances and learn from one's mistakes.
    Contrast culture: Making mistakes results in an unacceptable loss of face.

30. *Competition versus cooperation*
    U.S. culture: Competition contributes to high performance.
    Contrast culture: Competition leads to disharmony.

31. *Compartmentalized versus general criticism*
    U.S. culture: Job-related criticism rarely affects a person's private life.
    Contrast culture: Job-related criticism affects all aspects of the worker's feelings about self.

32. *Mobility versus continuity and commitment*
    U.S. culture: Geographic and career mobility (promotions) are to be sought.
    Contrast culture: Continuity and commitment are more important than mobility.

33. *Direct versus indirect questioning*
    U.S. culture: Direct questioning is the best way to get information.
    Contrast culture: Direct questioning is rude and intrusive.

34. *Direct answers versus softened responses*
    U.S. culture: Direct answers, even if they are negative, are efficient and tend to be respected.
    Contrast culture: Directly negative responses should be avoided because they cause loss of face and disharmony and are rude.

35. *Confrontation versus avoidance*
    U.S. culture: Interpersonal conflicts should be discussed directly.
    Contrast culture: Interpersonal conflicts should be glossed over.

36. *Informality versus formality*
    U.S. culture: Informality and casual appearance are signs of warmth and equality.
    Contrast culture: Informality can be intrusive and can result in loss of respect for a superior.

37. *Variety versus consistency of procedures*
    U.S. culture: Constant efforts should be made to find new and better ways to do tasks.
    Contrast culture: Once a procedure has been worked

out, it should not be changed unless it is absolutely necessary.

38. *Active versus passive learning*
U.S. culture: Learning is best accomplished through active participation.
Contrast culture: Learning can be accomplished without active participation.

39. *Creative thinking versus rote repetition*
U.S. culture: Information is best learned through the process of creative thinking.
Contrast culture: Information is best learned through rote repetition.

40. *Abbreviated versus flowery conversation*
U.S. culture: Conversation should be accomplished as efficiently and simply as possible. In business, flowery language is inappropriate and suspicious.
Contrast culture: Poetic conversation is a virtue and an art to be acquired.

41. *Words versus context*
U.S. culture: The meaning of a statement is generally based only on the words themselves.
Contrast culture: The meaning of a statement is based on the words along with the context of those words, which might include past conversations, body language, or the current social or professional relationship.

42. *Verbal versus nonverbal language*
U.S. culture: Verbal communication—the words themselves—is by far the most important component in the communication process.
Contrast culture: Words are only a small part of the communication process. Tone of voice and body language tell far more about the true meaning of what is being said.

Appendix G:
Sample Exercise—Focusing Attention

What Do I Want from This Program?

Following is a list of goals that this program is designed to achieve. Take a moment to rank each statement on a scale of 1–8, according to its importance to you today. Feel free to add any additional goals of your own.

I Hope To:

_____ Learn to communicate successfully in the face of accent and language differences

_____ Learn more about my own culture

_____ Learn to interpret accurately the behaviors of those who are different from me

_____ Learn to work efficiently with people of diverse cultural backgrounds

_____ Learn to feel more comfortable and confident in a multi-cultural environment

---

The format of this exercise is based on one found in George F. Simons, *Working Together* (Los Altos, Calif.: Crisp Publications, 1989).

_____ Learn to gain cooperation from those whose cultural background is different from my own

_____ Learn how to make people from other cultures feel more comfortable and function more effectively in the American workplace

_____ Learn to avoid applying stereotypes and prejudgments to other cultural groups

Add Goals of Your Own:

_____

_____

Appendix H:
Sample Exercise—Pretest

Cross-Cultural Awareness Assessment

Some of the following questions have more than one correct answer.

1. When I meet a worker who is a Central American immigrant, my first thought is that:
   a. Although Hispanic cultures are diverse, he or she is almost certainly Catholic and fond of big families like so many Mexicans I know.
   b. It is impossible to generalize about the values of any group.
   c. It is likely that he or she has more respect for authority than most native-born workers.

2. *True or false:* American culture has no unique characteristics. It is merely composed of features brought here by various immigrant groups.

3. When communicating with workers from other cultures, humor is:
   a. Always a common denominator that promotes warmth
   b. Sometimes dangerous because it can be misunderstood
   c. All right as long as the worker is laughing too

4. *True or false:* When adapting to a new country, the first

thing to change are the immigrant's behaviors; attitudes follow later.

5. A person who still has a foreign accent after being in this country for years probably:

   a. Does not understand much English
   b. Is uneducated
   c. Speaks a language that has different linguistic roots than English does

6. The concern with loss of face is a cultural doctrine found in:

   a. Asian cultures
   b. Hispanic cultures
   c. Middle Eastern, Asian, and Hispanic cultures

7. Immigrants who never go after promotions are probably:

   a. Uncommitted to the good of the company as a whole
   b. Good workers who enjoy doing their own job well
   c. Avoiding the promotions for cultural reasons

8. *True or false:* Culture shock usually strikes within the first few days of moving to a new country.

9. *True or false:* Behaving formally around immigrant workers—using last names, dressing nicely—is generally not a good idea, since it makes you seem cold and aloof.

10. Immigrant or ethnic workers who do not speak up with ideas in the training room or at meetings probably:

    a. Are afraid of making a mistake when they speak English
    b. Have no ideas because they do not understand American business practices
    c. Feel that it is disrespectful of authority to voice their own ideas
    d. Do not want to call attention to themselves

Answers
1. b and c
2. False

3. b
4. True
5. c
6. c
7. b and c
8. False
9. False
10. a, c, and d

Appendix I:
Sample Exercise—Language
Pretest

Bridging Language Barriers: An Exercise in Awareness

Some of the following questions have more than one correct answer.

1. Learning to speak a few words of the language of immigrant workers is:

   a. Generally not a good idea because they might feel patronized
   b. Generally not a good idea because they might be offended if a mistake in vocabulary or pronunciation is made
   c. Generally a good idea as the effort communicates respect for the other person

2. A good way to improve communication when a nonnative English speaker does not understand me is to:

   a. Speak louder because it makes it easier for the listener to decipher what I am saying
   b. Speak more slowly and distinctly
   c. Minimize gestures and facial expressions; they only create confusion by providing too many messages

d. Speak pidgin English; it is what most immigrants are accustomed to hearing

3. When the speaker with an accent sounds rude, I:

a. Realize that apparent rudeness can be related to language facility
b. Tend to take offense, just as I would with anyone else
c. Realize that some cultures have a more assertive manner than others

4. When communicating with nonnative English speakers, the use of jargon, slang, and idioms is:

a. Generally a good idea as this is an excellent way to familiarize the immigrant with this vocabulary
b. Generally not a good idea because it increases the chances of being misunderstood
c. Generally a good idea because it seems more friendly and easygoing

5. What is the best thing to do if you have trouble understanding what a foreign-born worker is saying?

a. Ask him or her to speak more slowly.
b. Paraphrase back what you think is being said.
c. Make an effort to listen more attentively.

6. When communicating across language barriers, using the written word:

a. Should be avoided; it can insult the immigrant's intelligence
b. Can be helpful; it is usually easier to read English than to hear it
c. Can be confusing; it is usually easier to hear English than to read it

7. *True or false:* I rarely, if ever, pretend to understand something when I do not.

8. In times of crisis, the immigrant's ability to speak English:

    a. Dimishes because of stress
    b. Stays the same
    c. Disappears
    d. Improves because of the necessity of coping with the crisis

9. When someone perpetually nods and smiles as I speak to him or her, it is:

    a. A good indication that he or she is paying attention
    b. An indication that he or she may not be understanding
    c. A good indication that I am being understood

10. When an immigrant worker fails to ask me any questions after I have given instructions, I:

    a. Feel that he or she cares little about what I have said
    b. Feel that he or she may not have understood enough to formulate a question
    c. Am confident that the material has gotten across
    d. realize that he or she may not have had enough time in which to formulate a question

Answers

1. c
2. b
3. a and c
4. b
5. a, b, and c
6. b
7. Probably false; we all do this.
8. a
9. b
10. b and d

Appendix J:
Sample Exercise—Action Plan

Action Plan: Taking It to The Workplace

Based on the material discussed in the program, please identify a cross-cultural issue in your workplace you would like to remedy.

Individuals involved (use pseudonyms or initials):

Objective:

Action:

Time frame (if appropriate):

Measures of Success:

Supplementary Reading

There are few books that deal specifically with how to manage the multicultural work force and still fewer that address these challenges as they are found within the boundaries of the United States. For this reason, many of the books listed here are international in focus or address themselves to the topic of cross-cultural communication in general. Although this does limit their applicability, they still contain much valuable information on cross-cultural communication, adaptation, values, etiquette, and management. Not all of these materials are in print, but most can be obtained at a university or large public library.

The categories under which these sources are arranged are intended as guidelines only. Many of them might be grouped under a number of different headings. Some of the books under "Cross-Cultural Training" for example, contain references to specific populations, and those found under the "General Culture and Cross-Cultural Management" category will certainly have considerable application to the design of cultural-awareness training programs.

Journal articles are not contained in this list. There do exist, however, many fine articles on the topics of managing and training the multicultural work force. They can be located by examining such management, human resources, training, and intercultural journals as the following: *Personnel Journal, Training and Development, Training, Personnel, Personnel Administrator, Public Personnel Management*, and *Supervisory Management*, and, on the intercultural side, the *International Journal of Intercultural Relations*. This last journal is published by the International Society for Intercultural Education, Training and Research (SIETAR). Readers interested in studying the history of and facts about various ethnic groups might read the *Journal of American Ethnic History* and/or the *Journal of Ethnic Studies.*

Several newsletters are particularly valuable to those who wish to become more involved in the issues of cultural diversity. These include: the *Training and Culture Newsletter Bulletin,* available from GilDeane Group, P.O. Box 82031, Kenmore, Washington 98028-0019, (206) 483-0755; the *Intercultural News Network,* available from the Pacific Area Communicator of Intercultural Affairs, 16331 Underhill Lane, Huntington Beach, California 92647, (714) 840-3688; and *Communique,* available from SIETAR, 733 Fifteenth Street, N.E., Suite 900, Washington D.C. 20005, (202) 737-5000.

Literature in the areas of international business, English-as-a-second-language training, educational materials for teachers who wish to instruct children in cross-cultural communication, foreign student services, and intercultural theory are also valuable resources for anyone who wishes to delve more deeply.

Associations and Presses

The following organizations are rich sources of information and publications on the topics of cross-cultural management and cultural diversity in general.

Brigham Young University, David M. Kennedy Center for International Studies, 280 HRCB, Provo, Utah 84602, (801) 378-6528.
Gulf Publishing Company, P.O. Box 2608, Houston, Texas 77001, (713) 529-4301.
Intercultural Press, P.O. Box 700, Yarmouth, Maine 04096, (207) 846-5168.
International Society for Intercultural Education, Training and Research (SIETAR), 733 Fifteenth Street, N.W., Suite 900, Washington D.C. 20005, (202) 737-5000.
Sage Publications, Inc., P.O. Box 5084, Newbury Park, California 91359, (805) 499-0721.

General Culture and Cross-Cultural Management

The following books can be consulted for information on the general topics of cross-cultural communication and management. In many cases, however, the work also contains references to specific population groups.

Asante, M.K., and W. Gudykunst, eds. *Handbook of International and Intercultural Communication*. Newbury Park, Calif.: Sage Publications, 1989.

Brislin, R. *Cross-Cultural Encounters: Face-to-Face Interaction*. New York: Pergamon Press, 1981.

———, K. Cushner, C. Cherrie, and M. Long. *Intercultural Interactions, A Practical Guide*. Beverly Hills: Sage Publications, 1986.

Condon, J., and F. Yousef. *An Introduction to Intercultural Communication*. New York: Macmillan, 1985.

Copeland, L., and L. Griggs. *Going International*. New York: Random House, 1985.

Gudykunst, W.B., S. Ting-Toomey, and E. Chua. *Culture and Interpersonal Communication*. Beverly Hills: Sage Publications, 1988.

Hall, E.T. *Beyond Culture*. Garden City, N.Y.: Anchor Press/Doubleday, 1981.

———. *The Silent Language*. Garden City, N.Y.: Doubleday, 1959.

Harris, P.R., and R.T. Moran, *Managing Cultural Differences*. 2d ed. Houston: Gulf Publishing Company, 1987.

Kessler, S. *Multicultural Management*. Fountain Valley, Calif.: Institute for Professional Training, 1981.

Kras, E. *Management in Two Cultures: Bridging the Gap between U.S. and Mexican Managers*. Yarmouth, Maine: Intercultural Press, 1989.

Language and Intercultural Research Center. *Intercultural Interacting*. Provo, Utah: Brigham Young University Center for International and Area Studies, 1977.

Moran, R.T., and P.R. Harris. *Managing Cultural Synergy*. Houston: Gulf Publishing Company, 1982.

Renwick, G., ed. *The Management of Intercultural Relations in International Business: A Directory of Resources*. Yarmouth, Maine: Intercultural Press, 1982.

Samovar, L.A., and R.E. Porter. *Intercultural Communication: A Reader*. 5th ed. Belmont, Calif.: Wadsworth Publishing Company, 1988.

_____, and N.C. Jain. *Understanding Intercultural Communication.* Belmont, Calif.: Wadsworth Publishing Company, 1981.

Sarbraugh, L.E. *Intercultural Communication.* New Brunswick, N.J.: Transaction Books, 1988.

Smith, E.C., and L. Luce, eds. *Toward Internationalism: Readings in Cross-Cultural Communication.* Rowley, Mass.: Newbury House Publishers, 1979.

Tyler, V.L. *Intercultural Interacting.* Provo, Utah: Intercultural Communicating, 1987.

Cross-Cultural Training

These books are useful in developing training programs on the topic of cross-cultural management. Many contain case studies, simulations, and exercises specially designed to aid the process of cultural-awareness training. There are also several books of exercises that are not intended specifically for diversity training but can be adapted to fit that purpose.

Batchelder, D., and E.G. Warner, eds. *Beyond Experience: The Experiential Approach to Cross-Cultural Education.* Brattleboro, Vt.: Experiment Press, 1977.

Casse, P. *Training for the Cross-Cultural Mind: A Handbook for Cross-Cultural Trainers and Consultants.* Washington D.C.: International Society for Intercultural Education, Training and Research, 1981.

_____. *Training for the Multicultural Manager.* Washington D.C.: International Society for Intercultural Education, Training and Research, 1982.

_____, and D. Surinder. *Managing Intercultural Negotiations.* Washington D.C.: International Society for Intercultural Education, Training and Research, 1985.

Feldman, M.J. *Coping with Problems in Meeting Training Needs for Cross-Cultural International Training.* Madison, Wis.: American Society for Training and Development, International Division, 1977.

Hoopes, D.S., and P. Ventura, eds. *Intercultural Sourcebook: Cross-Cultural Training Methodologies.* Yarmouth, Maine: Intercultural Press, 1979.

Kohls, R.L. *Developing Intercultural Awareness*. Washington D.C.: International Society for Intercultural Education, Training and Research, 1981.

_____. *Methodologies for Trainers: A Compendium of Learning Strategies*. Washington D.C.: International Society for Intercultural Education, Training and Research, 1979.

_____, ed. *Training Know-How for Cross-Cultural Trainers*. Washington D.C.: Washington International Center of Meridian House International, 1985.

Landis, D., and R. Brislin, eds. *Handbook of Intercultural Training*. 3 vols. Elmsford, N.Y.: Pergamon Press, 1983.

_____, and J. Martin. *Theories and Methods in Cross-Cultural Orientation*. Yarmouth, Maine: Intercultural Press, 1986.

Newman, J.W., and E.E. Scannell. *Games Trainers Play: Experimental Learning Exercises*. New York: McGraw-Hill, 1980.

Nitsche, R.A., and A. Green. *Situational Exercises in Cross-Cultural Awareness*. Columbus, Ohio: Charles E. Merrill Publishing Company, 1977.

Renwick, G.W. *Evaluation Handbook for Cross-Cultural Training and Multicultural Education*. Yarmouth, Maine: Intercultural Press, 1980.

Scannell, E.E., and J.W. Newstrom. *More Games Trainers Play*. New York: McGraw-Hill, 1983.

Seelye, H.N. *Teaching Culture: Strategies for Intercultural Communication*. Lincoln Wood, Ill.: National Textbook Company, 1985.

Simons, G.F. *Working Together: How to Become Effective in a Multicultural Organization*. U.S.A.: Crisp Publications, 1989.

Stewart, E.C., J. Danielian, and R. Foster. *Simulating Intercultural Communication through Role-Playing*. Alexandria, Va.: Humrro, 1969.

Weeks, W.H., P.B. Pedersen, and R.W. Brislin, eds. *A Manual of Structured Experiences for Cross-Cultural Learning*. Yarmouth, Maine: Intercultural Press, 1977.

Assorted Population Groups

The following works provide information about specific cultural groups. Some deal with several different groups, and others focus on only one population. Although most of these are international in focus, they are still helpful, although to a lessened extent, in helping us understand those groups as they are found within the United States. You will notice that included here are several works about mainstream American culture. These will help readers understand their own background in order to understand others.

Series

The following entries each represent a series of publications, each item of which deals with a different country.

Country Profiles. Available through Superintendent of Documents, Washington D.C. 20402. Several countries are available in the series.

Culturgrams. Available from the David M. Kennedy Center for International Studies, Brigham Young University, 280 HRCB, Provo, Utah 84602, (801) 378-6528. More than ninety-five countries are included in the series.

Doing Business in . . . Available from SRI International, Menlo Park, Calif. Fourteen countries are available.

InterActs. Available from Intercultural Press, P.O. Box 768, Yarmouth, Maine 04096, (207) 846-5168. *InterActs* have been published that deal with the following cultures: Arab, Australian, Japanese, Mexican, and Thai.

Bibliography

Kohls, L.R., and V.L. Tyler. *A Select Guide to Are Studies* Provo, Utah: David M. Kennedy Center for International Studies, Brigham Young University, 1988.

Individual Books

Almaney, A.J., and A.J. Alwan. *Communicating with the Arabs: A Handbook for the Business Executive* Prospect Heights, Ill.: Waveland Press, 1982.

Althen, G. *American Ways: A Guide for Foreigners.* Yarmouth, Maine: Intercultural Press, 1988.

Armour, M., P. Knudson, and I. Meeks. *The Indochinese: New Americans*. Provo, Utah: Brigham Young University Language Research Center, 1981.

Axtell, E., ed. *Do's and Taboos around the World*. New York: John Wiley & Sons, 1985.

Carroll, R. *Cultural Misunderstandings: The French-American Experience*. Chicago: University of Chicago Press, 1988.

Condon, J.C. *InterAct 1—Good Neighbors: Communicating with the Mexicans*. Yarmouth, Maine: Intercultural Press, 1985.

———. *InterAct 4—With Respect to the Japanese: A Guide for Americans*. Yarmouth, Maine: Intercultural Press, 1984.

David M. Kennedy Center for International Studies. *The Indochinese: New Americans*. Provo, Utah: Brigham Young University, 1981.

Deutsch, M.F. *Doing Business with the Japanese*. New York: New American Library, 1983.

Fieg, J.P. *InterAct 3—A Common Core: Thais and North Americans*. Yarmouth, Maine: Intercultural Press, 1989.

Hall, E.T., and M.R. Hall. *Understanding Cultural Differences: Germans, French, and Americans*. Yarmouth, Maine: Intercultural Press, 1990.

Kennedy, G. *Doing Business Abroad*. New York: Simon and Schuster, 1985.

Kochman, T. *Black and White Styles in Conflict*. Chicago: University of Chicago Press, 1981.

Lanier, A.R. *Living in the U.S.A.* Yarmouth, Maine: Intercultural Press, 1981.

MacLeod, R. *China, Inc.: How to Do Business with the Chinese*. New York: Bantam Books, 1988.

Nitsche, R.A., and A. Green. *Situational Exercises in Cross-Cultural Awareness*. Columbus, Ohio: Charles E. Merrill Publishing Company, 1977.

Nydell, M.K. *InterAct 5—Understanding Arabs: A Guide for Westerners*. Yarmouth, Maine: Intercultural Press, 1987.

Rowland, D. *Japanese Business Etiquette*. New York: Warner Books, 1985.

Sandoli, A. *New Americans: An Oral History*. New York: Viking Press, 1988.

Stewart, E.C. *American Cultural Patterns: A Cross-Cultural Perspective*. Yarmouth, Maine: Intercultural Press, 1972.

Wedge, B.M. *Visitors to the United States and How They See Us*. Princeton, N.J.: D. Van Nostrand, 1965.

Index

Accents, 40–1, 70, 71, 164, 199
Aggression, 8
American culture, 27–29, 160;
contrast with other cultures,
225–231; independent achievement
and, 163; proverbs as reflection
of, 29–32; teaching of, 34; values
of, 153
Anger, 92
Apologies, 118
Assimilation of foreign workers, 18
Authority: attitudes toward,
104–105, 107–113; confusion
about, 120; respect for, xx–xxi, 3,
112–113

Bacon, Francis, 145, 146
Behavior: etiquette and, 116;
interpretation, 101, 113, 151–153,
167 positive reinforcement of,
165–167; workplace, 146–147
Behavior changes and motivations,
113, 145–147; compromise and,
157–160; decision-making power
and, 150, 167; manager
expectations and, 153–156;
productivity and, 146
psychological safety and, 92, 147,
167, 174; reassurance techniques,
150; resistance to, 147–150
Benedict, Ruth, 23, 26
Bilingualism, 41
Body language, 67–68, 72, 77; eye
contact, 24, 67, 116, 135–136,
137; (table); gesturing, 51–52;
proximity of speakers, 117,
132–134, 135; touching, 134–135

Carlyle, Thomas, 49
Change. See Behavior changes and
motivations
Churchill, Winston, 65, 140
Communication, 2, 46–57, 201;
criticism and, 104; cross-cultural
(general discussion), 35, 51, 81;
language differences and, 37–38;
language etiquette and, 126–131;
lip movements and, xix, 72;
repetition in, 71; of respect, xxii,
14, 24, 26, 35, 160, 167, 204;
responsibility for, 71, 77; speed,
71, 72; spelling of difficult words,
71–72; telephone, 50–51; written
word, 68, 71, 77. See also Body
language
Community vs. the individual, xx
Competition, 99, 113, 163–164
Complaints, 155, 157–158, 165
Compliments, 116, 124–125
Compromises, 157–160, 167
Confirmation bias, 16
Conflict resolution, 201, 221–222
Confrontations, negative, 83–88
Consultants, 171–172
Criticism and negative statements,
92–93, 99, 104, 113, 134, 165;
guidelines for, 219–220; of
superiors, 112

About the Author

Dr. Sondra Thiederman is president of Cross-Cultural Communications, a San Diego-based training firm that offers programs on managing the multicultural work force, selling to the immigrant consumer, and delivering customer service across cultural and language barriers.

Since receiving her doctorate from UCLA, she has served as consultant to the Affirmative Action Department of the University of California, the American Cancer Society, and The Center for Indo-Chinese Health Education. Dr. Thiederman has also provided workshops and platform addresses for clients ranging from Rockwell International, Marriott Corporation, and Security Pacific National Bank to American Medical International, the Society for Human Resource Management, and Meeting Planners International.

Widely featured in the media, including the "Merv Griffin Show" and the *Los Angeles Times*, she has been published in such human resource and management journals as *Personnel Journal*, *The Journal of Staffing and Recruitment*, *Supervisory Management*, and *Training and Development Journal*. In addition to *Bridging Cultural Barriers for Corporate Success*, Dr. Thiederman is the author of a forthcoming book for the general public on how to do business in our multicultural society (Lexington Books 1991).